CAROL KOECHLIN / SANDI ZWAAN

TEACHING TOOLS

FOR THE INFORMATION AGE

Online Research (Library)
Ministry of Education & Training
13th Floor, Mowat Block, Queen's Park
Toronto, Ontario M7A 1L2

Pembroke Publishers Limited

© 1997 Pembroke Publishers Limited
538 Hood Road
Markham, Ontario L3R 3K9 Canada

All rights reserved.

No part of this publication may be reproduced in any form or by any means, electronic or mechanical, including photocopy, recording or any information or retrieval system, without permission in writing from the publisher.

Every effort has been made to contact copyright holders for permission to reproduce borrowed material. We regret any oversights that may have occurred and will be pleased to rectify them in subsequent reprints of the work.

Thanks to the following teachers from the Scarborough Board of Education for their review of the manuscript.

Ann Marie Fitzpatrick
Sandra Bassett
Janis Taylor
Pat Martingale
Hanny Lester
Joanne Clement
Denise White
Lynn Malandrino
Candace Ramdial
Liz Arkwright
Prince Duah
Dave Pollard
Azza Hamid

Canadian Cataloguing in Publication Data

Koechlin, Carol
    Teaching tools for the information age

(Information power)
Includes bibliographical references and index.
ISBN 1-55138-084-6

1. Study skills – Study and teaching (Primary).
I. Zwaan, Sandi. II. Title. III. Series.

LB1601.K63 1997   372.13'02'81   C97-931427-5

Editor: Alan Simpson
Cover Design: John Zehethofer
Cover Photography: Ajay Photographics
Typesetting: Jay Tee Graphics Ltd.
Printed and bound in Canda

9 8 7 6 5 4 3 2

Teaching Tools will help you guide students through group and independent research projects. It provides information and tools to facilitate student self-, peer and group evaluation in addition to formative, ongoing assessment and summative evaluation. It will assist students in setting goals for learning and managing their time effectively.

Reproducible pages deal with curriculum extensions, and offer cross-curricular and integration tools and graphic organizers that will save valuable preparation time.

This icon identifies the pages in this book that you have permission to copy for classroom use.

Contents

Introduction *5*

The Knowledge Economy *5*
Information Literacy *5*
Skills Needed for Lifelong Learning *6*
Learning to Learn *6*
Developing Curriculum to Promote Information Literacy Skills *6*
Using This Resource *6*
Intellectual Access to Information *7*

1 Define and Clarify Information Needs *8*

A Plan for Research Success *9*
Information Literacy: Planning for Integration *11*
Student Progress – Steps to Success *14*
Exploration *15*
Reflecting and Making Personal Connections *15*
Talking About It *16*
Brainstorming *16*
Clustering *17*
Webbing *17*
Focusing on a Research Topic *18*
Questioning *18*
Questioning for Older Students *19*
Focusing and Organizing a Data Search *22*
Tools for Accessing Information *23*
Starting a Research Folder *23*

2 Locate and Retrieve Resources from a Variety of Sources *24*

Discovering Resources *25*
Using the Library Information Centre *25*
Ready to Search *27*
Locating Materials — Scavenger Hunt *27*
The Survey Process *32*
Interviewing *34*
Connecting to Human Resources *34*

3 Select, Process and Record Relevant Data *35*

Selecting Data *36*
Reading Pictures *36*
Listening *38*
Viewing *39*
Reading *40*
Collecting Information *42*
Fact and Fiction *44*
Recording Data *45*
Dot-Jot Notes *46*
Student-Designed Organizers *52*
Recording Sources *53*
Student Self-Assessment *53*

4 Analyse and Synthesize Information *55*

Synthesis *56*
Practising Analysis and Synthesis *57*
Using Graphic Organizers to Develop Thinking Skills *59*
Focus Words *60*
Higher-Level Thinking Skills *61*
Series Lines or Time Lines *62*
Webs *62*
Venn Diagrams *63*

T Charts *63*
Cross-Classification Charts *64*
Tree Diagrams *64*

5 Share and Use Learning *65*

Answering Questions and Sharing Learning *66*
Creating Something New *66*
Further Presentation Ideas *67*
Considering Multiple Intelligences *67*
Developing Skills Self-Awareness *69*
Planning Presentations *69*
Share Your Talents *72*
Presentation Cube *73*
Writing for Various Purposes and Audiences *74*
Writing Process *74*
Evaluation *74*
Presentation Rubric – Peer Evaluation *78*

6 Engage in Literary and Media Experiences *79*

Personal Selection Criteria *80*
Helping Students Make Personal Connections *80*
Critical Thinking *80*
Learning About Yourself *85*
Reflecting on Feelings Using Time Lines *86*
Connecting Reading, Viewing, Writing *86*
Prediction *86*
Problems and Solutions *86*
Story Mapping *87*
Comparing Versions *92*
Analysis *92*
Deconstructing Media *92*
Using Literature to Develop Thinking Skills *95*
Problem Solving *95*
Fluency and Flexibility *96*
Decision Making *96*
Sequencing and Story Mapping *97*

Clothesline Story *97*
Using Video to Develop Thinking, Visual and Language Skills *98*

7 Reflect on, Transfer and Apply Learning *100*

Making Skills Connections *101*
Transferring Skills and Thinking Critically *101*
Analysing Resources *101*
Lifelong Learning *101*
Modelling Problem Solving Skill Transference *102*
Student Portfolios *103*
Reflection Starters *103*
Reflection Tools *104*
  Sharing Reflections *104*
  Conferencing *104*
  Working Together *104*
  At Home *104*
Tracking and Evaluation *110*
Student Self- and Peer Evaluation *110*
Tracking Students' Abilities *114*

At Each Stage … *115*

Using Technologies to Enhance Learning *117*
Comparing Technologies *118*
Technical Tips *119*
Click on a CD-ROM *120*
Be WEBwise *121*
Words for the WEBwise *122*
© Copyright Alert *123*
Computer Learning Log *124*

In Conclusion *125*

Related Resources *126*

Index *127*

Introduction

The world of work and pleasure is changing rapidly. We live in the midst of an information revolution. As quickly as technology is developing, knowledge is expanding even more swiftly. We are deluged by information from a broad range of sources, including traditional print and electronic media and the newer media along the information highway. Information is increasing at lightning speed. Consider this: The total body of knowledge is currently doubling every 3.5 years and we are told that by the year 2040 it will likely double about every 78 hours. This is truly an explosion of information, and it will have a profound effect on the world around us. It also affects not just *how* but *what* we teach our students.

The Knowledge Economy

Futurists in North America predict that within ten years almost half of the workforce will be employed in the data services — gathering, processing, retrieving and/or analysing information. To be successful in this information economy, students must prepare themselves with the knowledge, skills and values that they'll need in tomorrow's world of work.

Educators around the world are grappling with developing curriculum to provide students with the skills they will need to be successful in the new millennium. We aren't even certain what students will need to know. What we do know is that learners must be able to handle vast amounts of information and deal with continual change. Alvin Toffler tells us that the illiterate of the year 2000 will not be those who cannot read and write but those who cannot learn, unlearn and relearn. Our students will need to be information literate, lifelong learners.

Information Literacy

A person who is information literate possesses both the technological and personal tools to locate information quickly and sift what's useful and current from what isn't.

Students who are information literate know how to learn. They know how to find information and how to use it. They locate information from a variety of sources: books, magazines, newspapers, television, radio, video, CD-ROMs and the Internet, in addition to classroom discussion, interviews with experts, and so on. Information literate students know how to select only the data they need from all the available sources. They process and record this data so that they can analyse and synthesize it. Information literate students are able to share what they have learned so that others can learn through them. They share and apply what they have learned through a variety of oral, written and multimedia presentations. They engage in literary and media experiences. Above all, they are aware of their own learning processes, they can reflect on, transfer and apply their learning. They are lifelong learners.

Skills Needed for Lifelong Learning

People who are lifelong learners are able to

- ☆ think critically
- ☆ solve problems
- ☆ work cooperatively and collaboratively
- ☆ process and manage information
- ☆ use technologies effectively
- ☆ apply knowledge to new situations
- ☆ take initiative
- ☆ take responsibility for their own learning

Learning to Learn

Learning to learn is a process of developing skills and gaining independence in their application. When students make connections between skills they have learned in school and how those skills transfer to real-life situations, they are well on their way to becoming lifelong learners. As teachers, we can facilitate that development by challenging our students to make the transfer. When we model this through integrated studies, our students experience authentic connections that are relevant and realistic. *Teaching Tools* provides resources for integrating information literacy, information technology and thinking skills.

Developing Curriculum to Promote Information Literacy Skills

Information literacy skills are the new basic. They provide the framework for lifelong learning. There isn't time in the school day to add yet another subject. Past experience has shown that skills taught in isolation are, at best, ineffectively transferred. We as teachers must inculcate and integrate these very important skills into existing curriculum.

The theme or topic for a unit of study accommodates more than knowledge of the subject. It supplies a vehicle for authentic integration of information literacy, thinking skills and information technologies. Often a unit includes a project or research assignment, but the students seldom have the prerequisite skills to do what is expected. The project or research assignment often assumes that students have acquired these skills. Until recently however, information literacy skills were not formally addressed in curriculum. Creating or adapting curriculum to integrate the teaching and practising of all the literacy skills is a real challenge.

Using This Resource

Teaching Tools was designed to simplify that process for you the teacher. It provides a complete and comprehensive compendium of teaching and learning strategies for information literacy. These strategies can be used with elementary school children at all grades.

Processing information is relevant for all ages. Some of the strategies and activities presented may be more appropriate for younger children, while others may be more suitable for older students. *Teaching Tools* identifies which strategies and activities are most appropriate for specific age levels. It will also assist you in providing and adapting learning experiences to satisfy a variety of student needs and multiple intelligences.

Each section provides strategies for building information literacy skills as students use a variety of media formats, participate in conferencing, work together and turn homework responsibility into a great game. This resource is designed to demonstrate the importance of process and the development by modelling of each stage in the process. Its aim is to assist you the teacher in helping students go beyond **physical access** of information to **intellectual access**.

Intellectual Access to Information

Accessing information intellectually requires that students develop and apply information literacy skills. This process is not strictly linear however; it contains recursive and overlapping elements. It is important that you the teacher model each step in the process.

The following graphic outlines the process of gaining intellectual access to information.

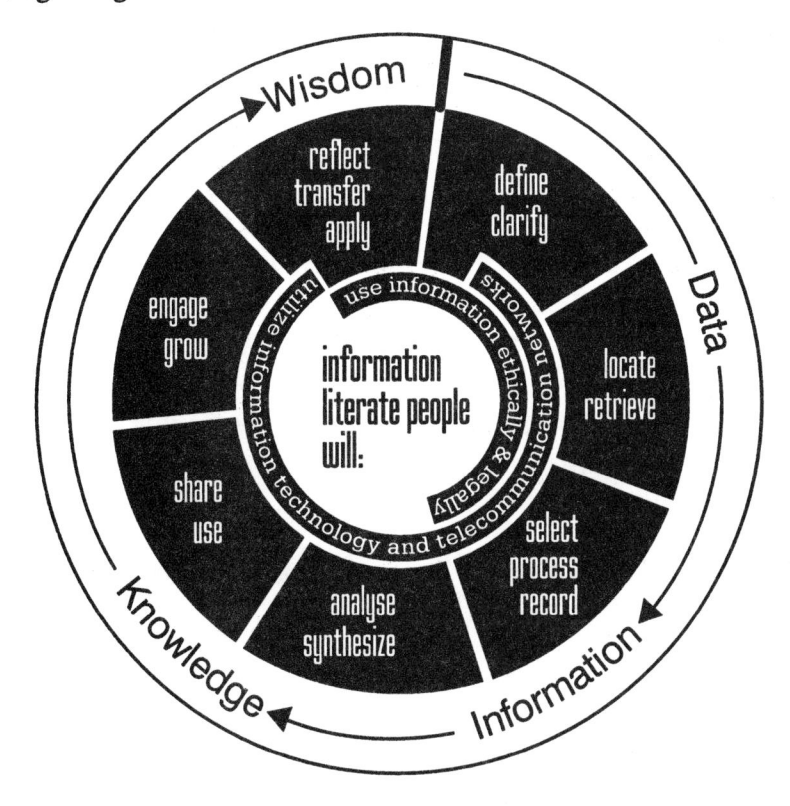

Data is a collection of raw facts.

The process of organizing and analysing data produces **information**.

The process of synthesizing this information and using one's own ideas to create something new leads to **knowledge** and **wisdom**.

1

Define and Clarify Information Needs

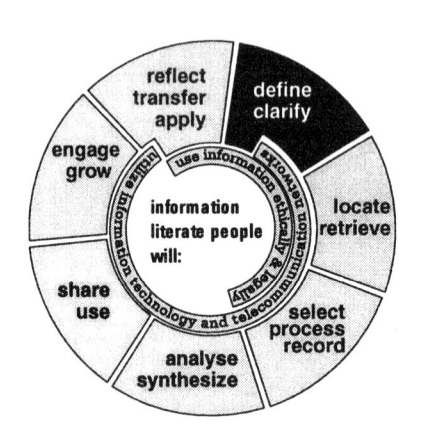

Before students can use information effectively, they must have a clearly defined purpose for their task.

Students can explore a topic using

☆ books, videos, pictures, the Internet, field trips
☆ interviewing, surveying

They focus on the topic by

☆ brainstorming, clustering and webbing ideas
☆ narrowing or broadening the topic so that it is manageable and meaningful

Students formulate an inquiry question or statement of purpose by

☆ using question starters
☆ identifying keywords

They identify ideas and subtopics to explore by

☆ brainstorming for "what I want to know"
☆ listing keywords for searches

Students create an action plan by

☆ using tracking sheets
☆ recording assignment requirements and due dates*
☆ listing the best places and methods for obtaining the required data
☆ listing people who can assist
☆ planning how to organize the gathered data*
☆ maintaining a research folder
☆ conferencing with the teacher and/or teacher-librarian and peers

---

* Younger students will need assistance in doing this.

A Plan for Research Success

The research process is an experience that students of all ages and abilities can engage in. It builds on a child's natural curiosity. The research process is far more than finding "all about" a topic. The misunderstandings educators have about research has led to "cut" and "paste" types of products and concerns about student plagiarism. The real problem here lies not with the student but with the design of the project. If we want them to learn more than isolated facts about animals, plants, famous people or whatever the content vehicle may be, then we must help students make connections and find personal meaning in the research topic. *Teaching Tools* will give you many strategies for helping students to focus on a manageable topic and define their information needs.

Researching is a collaborative process that requires cooperative planning, guidance and conferencing between the teacher and teacher-librarian and the student. It is advisable for very young students to work together to support each other during the process.

Although the skills required to access information intellectually are clearly defined, the process is not linear. There is a great deal of overlapping. For instance, when students are selecting materials that are appropriate for their research needs, they are actually practising analysis (in stage 4). Evaluation (stage 7) is ongoing throughout the process.

The research process gives students information power.

The visual representation on the following page demonstrates graphically four stages of the research process.

At each stage, you will guide your students through a variety of skill-development activities which prepare them for the next stage in the process.

Although this book is organized by learning expectations, these learnings may be introduced and practised at many points in the process. The suggested activities can be adapted to apply to many other curriculum areas. Indeed, we need to assist students in applying their information literacy skills in all curriculum areas if they are to have opportunities for real transference.

The research process naturally encompasses and integrates

☆ time management
☆ cooperative learning
☆ thinking
☆ subject content
☆ traditional literacy
☆ numerical literacy
☆ information technology
☆ information literacy

A Plan for Research Success

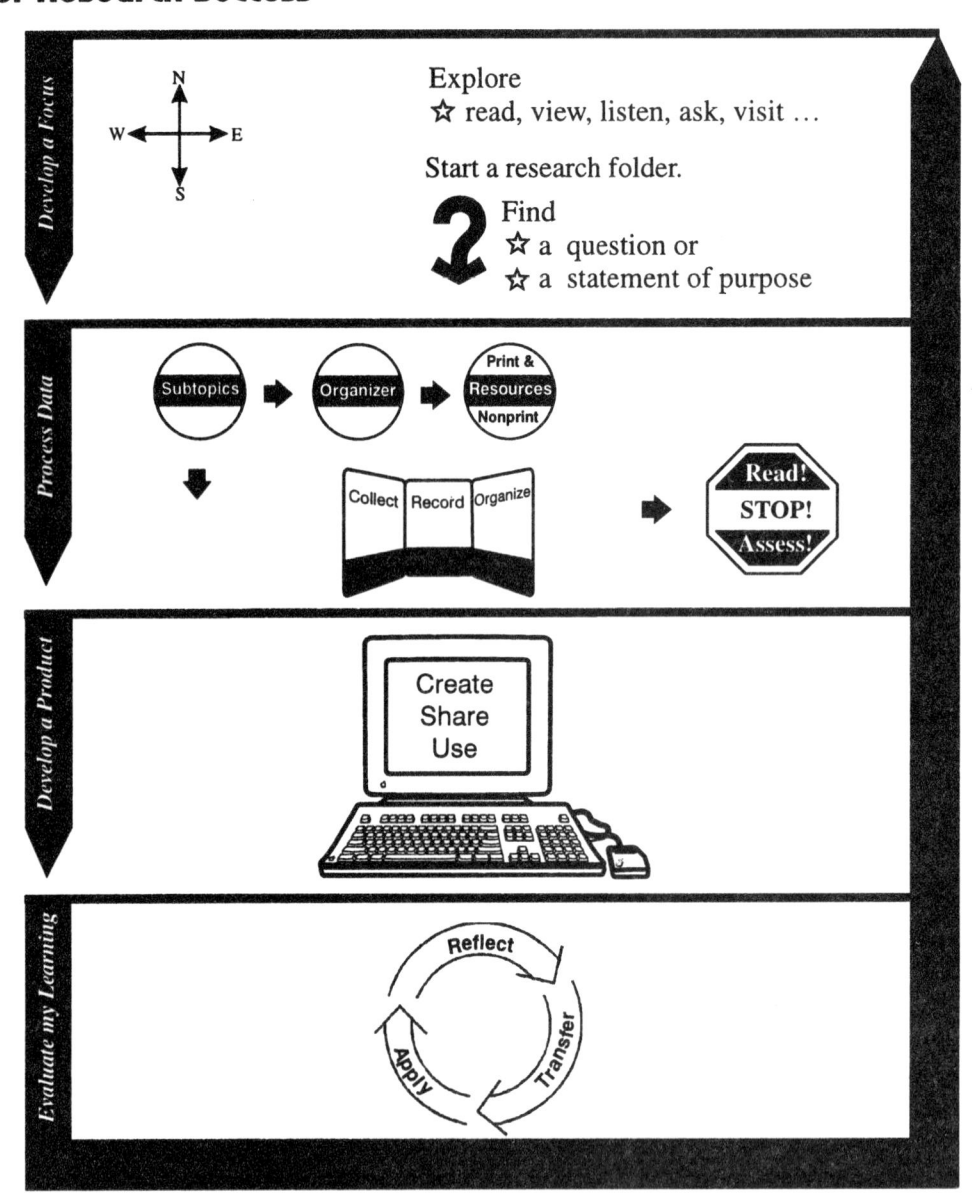

Develop a Focus

Explore
☆ read, view, listen, ask, visit ...

Start a research folder.

Find
☆ a question or
☆ a statement of purpose

Process Data

Subtopics → Organizer → Print & Nonprint Resources

Collect | Record | Organize

Read! STOP! Assess!

Develop a Product

Create Share Use

Evaluate my Learning

Reflect • Transfer • Apply

The Teacher Planning Sheets on pages 11 to 13 are designed to help you prepare for each stage of the research process. Your teacher-librarian is your school's information specialist and will be a valuable partner in planning, teaching and evaluating during the process.

Student Progress

You can use the organizer on page 14 to keep track of student progress during the research process. You may wish to enlarge it to poster size so that students can see their progress. Using icons regularly will help students transfer skills.

Information Literacy:

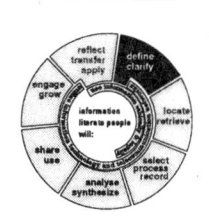

Planning for Integration

Planning for Integration	Teacher _____
	Teacher-librarian _____
Topic/Theme _____	

Questions for Preplanning	**Notes/Responsibilities**
Which student learnings are being targeted (cross-curricular and subject-specific)? What topic or theme will provide the vehicle for learning? How much time do you have? Who are the special-needs children? What are their needs? What skills need to be pretaught? Where will the learning take place?	

Developing a Focus	**Notes/Responsibilities**
What exploratory activities will introduce the unit? What activities will help students define and clarify their needs? (Establish keywords, develop questions.) What are the indicators? How will I know when students are ready to proceed?	

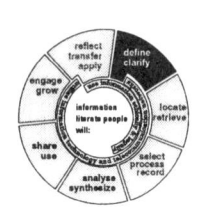

Processing Data	**Notes/Responsibilities**
What resources will children have access to?	
Do they have the prerequisite location and retrieval skills?	
Do students have selection criteria and search strategies?	
How will I structure the use of organizers?	
How will I assist students to develop subtopics?	
How will I know students can select, process and record relevant information? (Indicators)	

Developing a Product	**Notes/Responsibilities**
What will I have students do to help them make personal meaning of their recorded data?	
What will students do to analyse and synthesize their gathered information?	
How will students communicate their learning?	
What will be the criteria for the sharing/product?	
What materials should I have available?	
How will I organize the sharing (time, space, audiences, food, etc.)?	

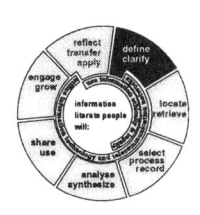

Evaluation	Notes/Responsibilities
What will be evaluated? How will evaluation take place? How will students self-evaluate? How will I evaluate the unit?	
Follow-up	**Notes/Responsibilities**
What opportunities will students have to transfer their skills into other curriculum areas? What opportunities will students have to extend their learning?	
Preparation Plan	**Notes/Responsibilities**
• • • • • •	

Steps to Success

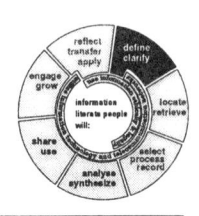

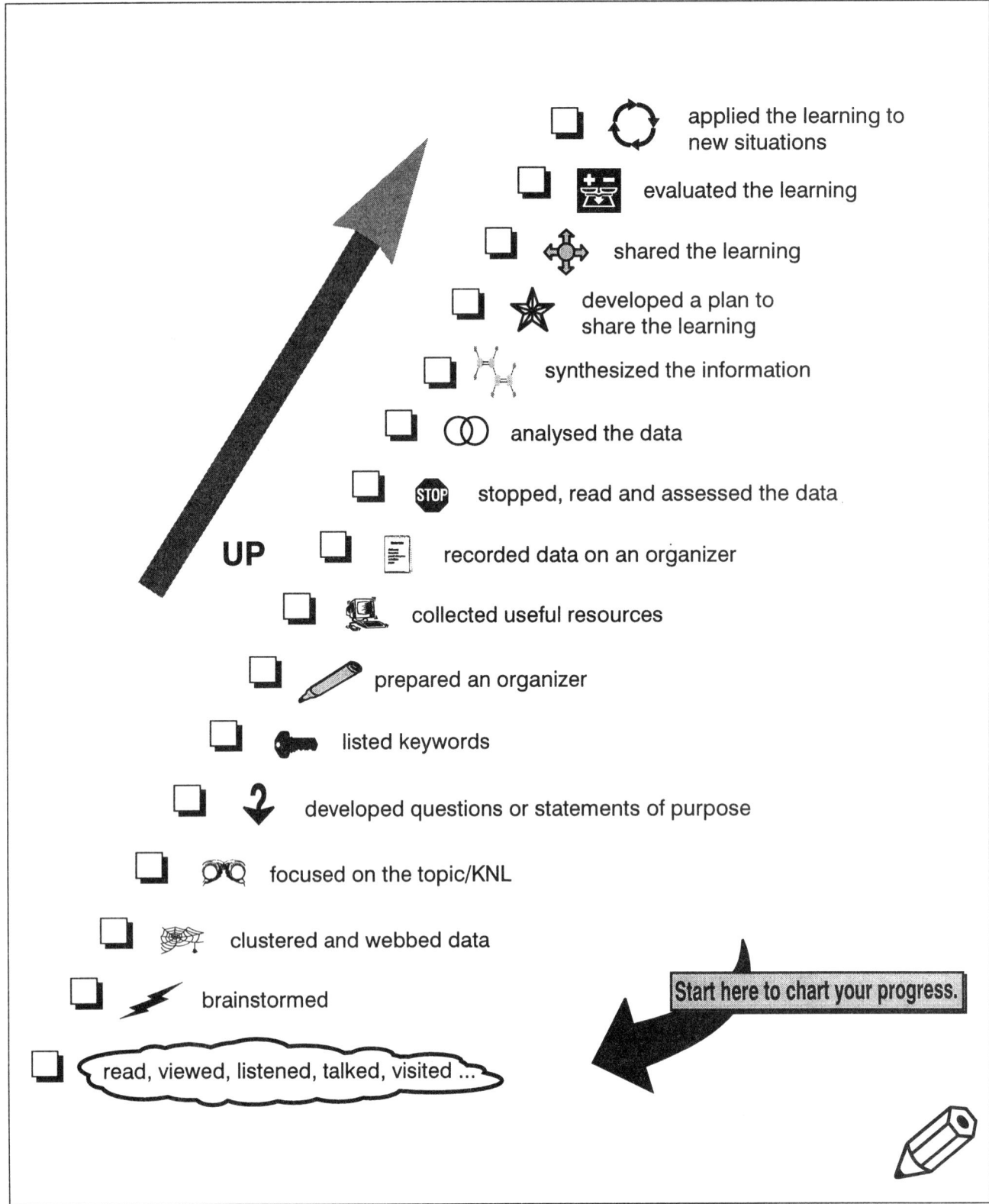

- ☐ applied the learning to new situations
- ☐ evaluated the learning
- ☐ shared the learning
- ☐ developed a plan to share the learning
- ☐ synthesized the information
- ☐ analysed the data
- ☐ stopped, read and assessed the data
- ☐ recorded data on an organizer
- ☐ collected useful resources
- ☐ prepared an organizer
- ☐ listed keywords
- ☐ developed questions or statements of purpose
- ☐ focused on the topic/KNL
- ☐ clustered and webbed data
- ☐ brainstormed
- ☐ read, viewed, listened, talked, visited ...

UP

Start here to chart your progress.

Exploration

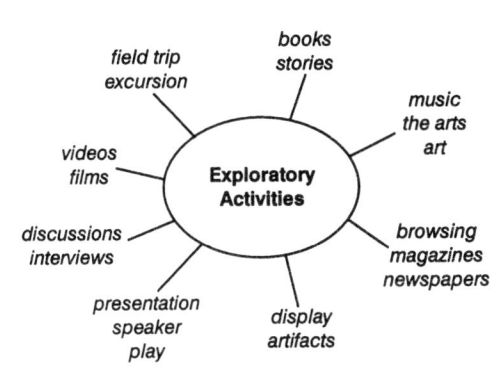

You have selected a theme as the vehicle for learning. Now students require a rich background of experiences with the topic to explore it thoroughly. This exploration stage must include a wide range of media to address multiple intelligences of all the students.

Although exploration is the most important step in the process, it is often erroneously omitted. It is during the exploratory stage that students acquire sufficient experience with the subject to peak their curiosity and desire to learn. They will gain a working knowledge of related vocabulary and basic content. These common experiences help level the playing field for the students and enable the teacher to guide them through collaborative focusing activities. The web illustrates the variety of broad exploratory activities students can undertake at this stage.

Reflecting and Making Personal Connections

As you facilitate these preresearch activities, encourage your students to reflect on the experiences and make personal connections. Ask them

☆ What do you see?
☆ What do you hear?
☆ What do you feel?
☆ What do you think about it?
☆ What do you wonder about?
☆ What are you curious about?
☆ What would you like to learn more about?

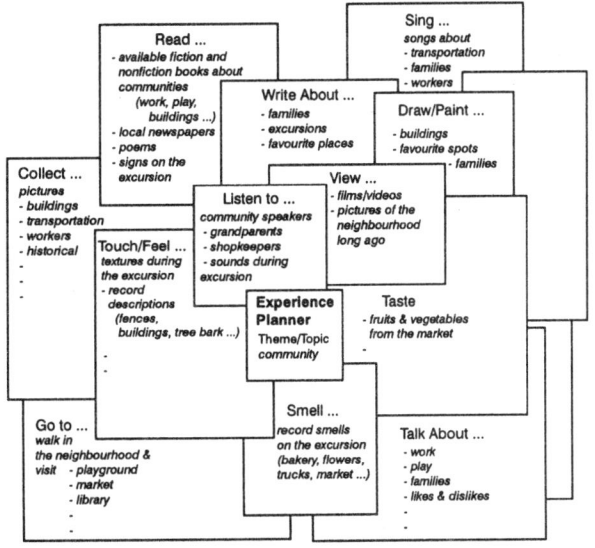

Students have had opportunities to

☆ explore
☆ discover
☆ listen
☆ ask
☆ discuss
☆ survey
☆ find
☆ observe
☆ identify
☆ try
☆ collect
☆ interview

Sharing
We think that ...

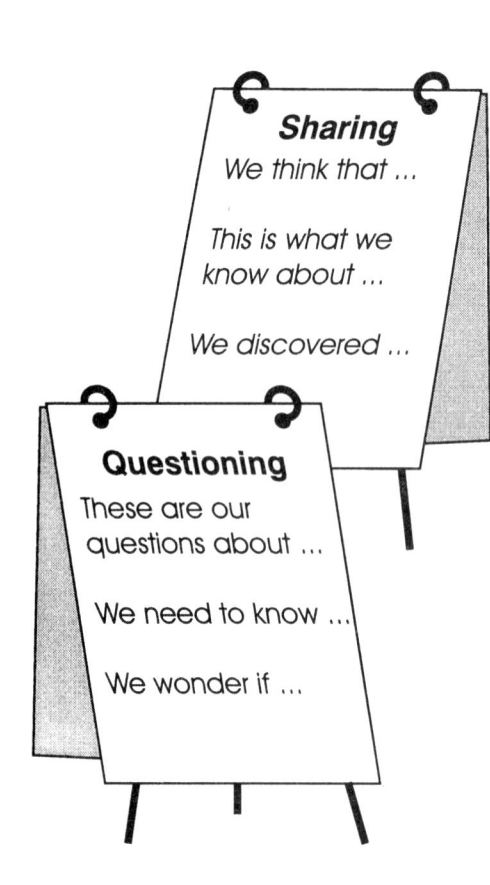

This is what we know about ...

We discovered ...

Questioning
These are our questions about ...

We need to know ...

We wonder if ...

The more experiences students have with the topic before the actual research begins, the more successful the research will be.

Talking About It

Primary students, especially, need many opportunities to talk about their learning. Before students can select an area of interest for their own personal or group research, you need to give them opportunities to record and classify the data they have so far.

To facilitate the talk and exploration you can

☆ use charts to record student discussion
☆ post charts and refer to them as the unit progresses
☆ accept all ideas
☆ revisit charts later to reassess, confirm or correct

Model **telling** and **questioning** with lots of experiences in safe large and small group situations.

Brainstorming

You can model brainstorming with the whole group and record on large charts the discoveries made so far. Post these charts around the room so that students have a physical reminder of their new learning. Teach the guidelines for brainstorming from the chart below.

Brainstorm for Bright IDEAS

Invite lots of ideas
  Go for quantity.
  From quantity comes quality.

Defer decisions
  Do not use putdowns.
  Don't make positive or negative judgments.

Expand!
  Piggyback or hitchhike on the ideas of others.

Accept all suggestions
  Add everything to your list.

Stretch thinking
  Be original.
  Try different ways, seek a new combination.

Brainstorming is a thinking exercise.
It is a way of getting lots and lots of ideas in a hurry.
It is a way of creating new ideas.
Students can brainstorm   individually
              with a friend
              in small groups
              with the class
Record all ideas on paper, charts, chalk board, sticky notes, computer ...

Clustering

You have explored the topic with your students.

Now you can assist the students in taking all the data and ideas gathered so far and looking for common threads by sorting, categorizing and classifying. Younger students will need lots of clustering experience in manipulating concrete materials before they begin using words and phrases. Try these clustering ideas!

Use coloured markers to circle common ideas. This would be a good time to introduce the term *subtopic*.

Try cutting all the rows of data apart. Now regroup them and paste on another chart, arranged in subtopics.

For nonreaders, use lots of sketches and few words when you brainstorm.

Webbing

Now that you have brainstormed and clustered, make a class web or mind map. This will help students to sort out what they have learned so far. For example:

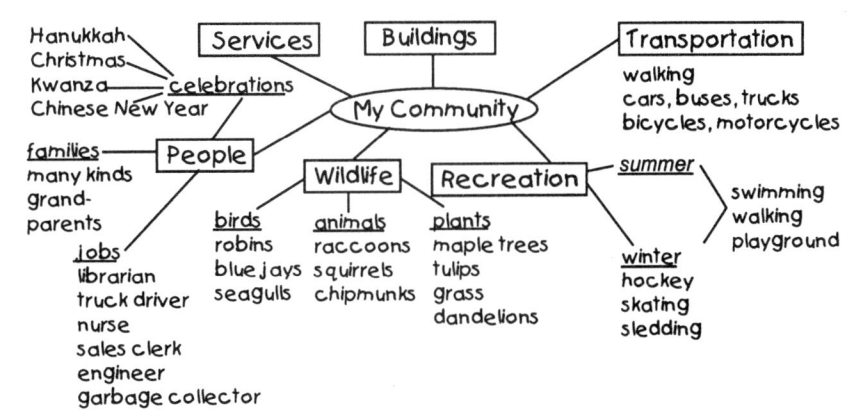

```
Hanukkah                                              Transportation
Christmas    Services    Buildings                    walking
Kwanza      celebrations                              cars, buses, trucks
Chinese New Year        My Community                  bicycles, motorcycles
families   People                                     summer
many kinds         Wildlife   Recreation                    swimming
grand-                                                       walking
parents      birds      animals    plants                    playground
   jobs      robins     raccoons   maple trees      winter
  librarian  blue jays  squirrels  tulips           hockey
  truck driver seagulls chipmunks  grass            skating
  nurse                            dandelions       sledding
  sales clerk
  engineer
  garbage collector
```

The students will be amazed at how much they already know. It will be easy for them to identify a smaller topic that they wish to explore further.

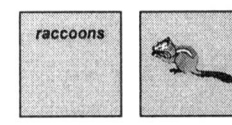

After a few experiences webbing in a large group, your students will be ready to form smaller groups to create their own webs. If individual ideas are recorded on sticky notes, it will be easy to move the notes around to group and regroup the ideas.

When a final organization for the web has been decided, glue the stickies in place and save the chart for future reference during the research process.

Focus on My Topic
Chinese New Year

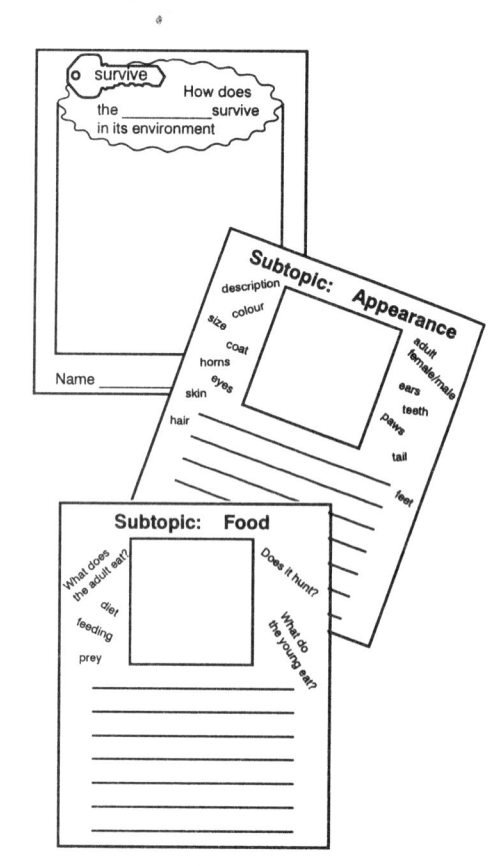

What I know!
- parades
- dragon dance
- gifts
- animal names are given to the year
- special food

What I need to know!
- How long does the celebration last?
- What things can children do?
- What do the animals mean for each year?
- How do you make the beautiful dragons?
- Are there other cultures that celebrate New Years at different times of the year?

Focusing on a Research Topic

Now take a close look at the web of the broad topic to help students find a smaller, more manageable focus for small-group or individual research. Younger students and nonreaders will need a great deal of help throughout the process. This affords a wonderful opportunity to pair up students with a learning buddy.

From the sample broad topic "My Community" we have chosen Chinese New Year for the focus of research in the following example. Using a chart like the one here, encourage your students to record everything they know about their topic and everything they would like to know about it. When working with very young or inexperienced children, you may want to do this as a group activity.

The focus worksheet will help students generate lots of ideas for creating their own inquiry question, selecting keywords for data searches and defining subtopics to organize their data.

Questioning

Primary students are innately curious about the world around them, but their questions are usually small and narrow and can be answered in a word or two. They require much help in learning to develop larger questions. In the beginning stages, you select the focus word or words for them. The whole class may be working on the same question but with different topics.

For example, if you are working on a study of wildlife in your local area, you might select the focus word *survive*. Students could develop their own questions based on the creature they have selected.

How does the _____ survive in its environment?

Everyone could work on the same question pattern, but each student or group would have their own animal.

Identifying Keywords

Good keywords are crucial to the success of an information search. In these examples the keywords and phrases were given to the students. Learning to identify effective keywords is a skill that comes with lots and lots of

KNowLedge

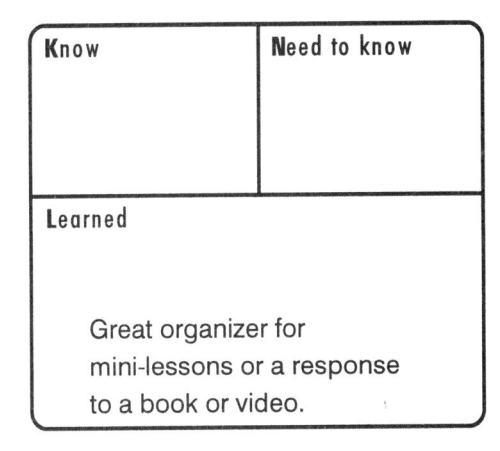

Know	Need to know

Learned

Great organizer for mini-lessons or a response to a book or video.

Defining My Needs

TOPIC_____ NAME_____

HOW	?
WHO	?
WHAT	?
WHEN	?
WHERE	?
WHY	?

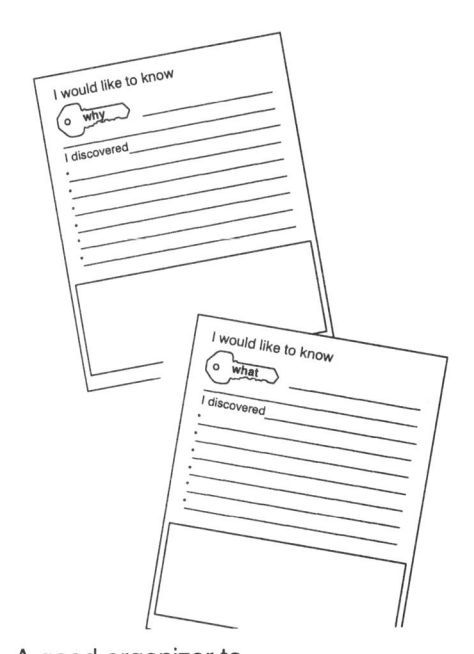

A good organizer to teach questioning skills.

experience. In the beginning, students may work in a group to develop a set of keywords to use in their search of indexes, tables of content and databases. They should be prepared to go back and choose other words should their search be unfruitful.

Developing Good Inquiry Questions

We as teachers have the opportunity to empower students to create research projects that are exciting and meaningful. We can bring an end to the tendency to just locate and regurgitate. By using effective inquiry questions or statements of purpose, students can move beyond simply collecting data to making personal meaning and relevance from them.

Question Starters

Employing the powerful words *Who, What, When, Where, Why* and *How* provides the best way for young researchers to start developing questioning skills. Again, extensive modelling is necessary.

Using graphic organizers will give your students practice in creating research questions.

Ensure that the students understand the meaning of each of the focus words listed on page 20. Encourage them to enlarge the lists by adding their own words. Model using these words in questions at every opportunity so that they become part of your students' working vocabulary.

Questioning for Older Students

By the time students have entered the junior years they should be ready to develop higher-level questions.

Questioning is a skill that requires practice. The following sample worksheets offer your students experiences in creating research questions. In these sheets, the topic of research is the mudskipper (a tropical fish that can survive on land) and its ability to adapt to its environment.

Use focus words from the activity sheets and post them in creative ways in the classroom. Select one or two focus words to concentrate on in a unit of study.

Questioning

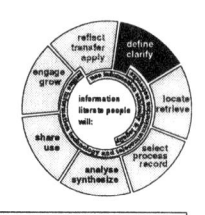

Questioning is a skill that takes practice.

Experiment with all kinds of questions until you find the one that is most interesting for you.

Here are some words to help you build good questions.

Starter Words for Questions

Who   What   When   Where   How   Why

Starter Words for Statements of Purpose

Investigate   Compare   Discover

Focus Words

Try using one or more of these powerful words to focus your question or statement:

changes	characteristics	types
kinds	roles	causes
effects	purpose	lifestyle
jobs	value	defence
importance	function	survival
structure	adapt	conditions

Questions and Statements of Purpose

Simple questions can be answered with

☆ Yes or No
☆ one-word answers
☆ facts only

If you want quick, short answers, use simple questions:

What colour is the mudskipper?

Where does a mudskipper live?

What does a mudskipper eat?

A mudskipper is one of many unusual creatures that depend on a healthy tropical wetland environment to survive.

Research questions will

☆ stimulate your curiosity
☆ challenge you to think about what you discover
☆ encourage you to dig deep for great information
☆ guide your whole research project
☆ focus your investigation

If you want rich rewards, use research questions:

Why is a tropical wetland a good habitat for a mudskipper?

How does a mudskipper **adapt** to **survive** in its environment?

How does the **structure** of a mudskipper **compare** with that of a frog?

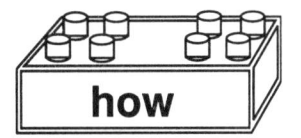

survive   **adapt**   **how**

Statements of purpose are also good research guides.

You may want to

Discover the **characteristics** of mudskippers.

Investigate the **role** of a mudskipper in a wetlands food chain.

Compare the life cycles of frogs and mudskippers.

21

Focusing and Organizing A Data Search — Keywords and Subtopics

Topic: *Mudskipper*

Question: *How does the mudskipper adapt to survive in its environment?*

Before beginning to collect data, students need some **keywords.**

Keywords are used to search

☆ indexes
☆ tables of content
☆ library catalogues
☆ CD-ROMs
☆ encyclopedias
☆ Internet Web sites

To find good keywords students look at their

☆ brainstorming
☆ webs
☆ mind maps

Next, decide on the **subtopics** to help organize the data students discovered.

What are subtopics?

☆ small pieces of the big topic
☆ pieces that will help students get the information they need to answer their question

topic - mudskipper

subtopics
- environment
- physical features
- life cycle
- food

How do students decide on subtopics?
They look for **clusters** and **strands** in their webs and mind maps.
They check their brainstorming, keywords, focus sheet, question.

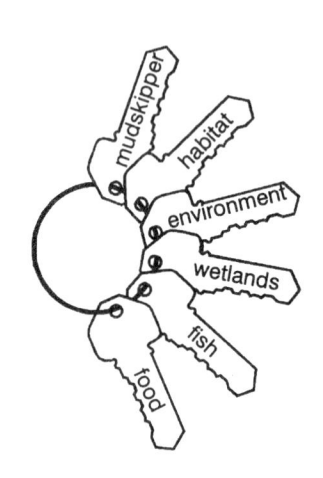

Tools for Accessing Information

Students can use tools like these to improve their success in defining and clarifying their information needs and tracking their progress as learners. You will find reproducible tracking and evaluation sheets in Chapter 7 (pages 111 to 114).

Starting a Research Folder

Now would be a good time for students to create a research folder. They will find it a valuable place to store resources and ideas they can use later in the process.

Why bother?

To help you organize.

To keep track of what is done and what needs to be done.

To help the teacher or teacher-librarian help you.

To document the research process for evaluation.

Where do I get a folder?

Make one!

Buy one.

Ask your teacher for a file folder.

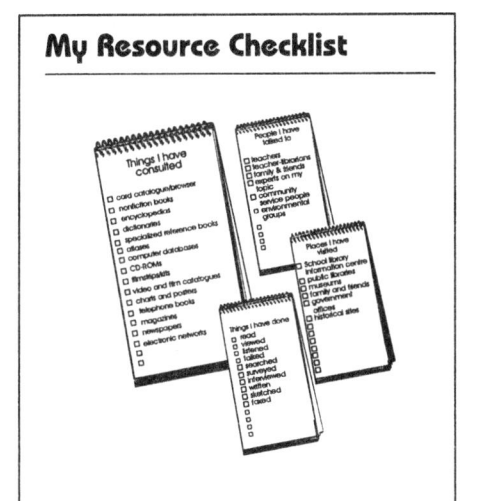

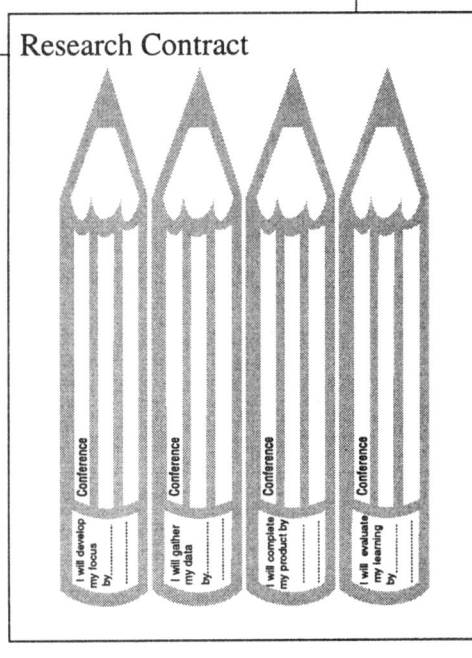

2

Locate and Retrieve Resources from a Variety of Sources

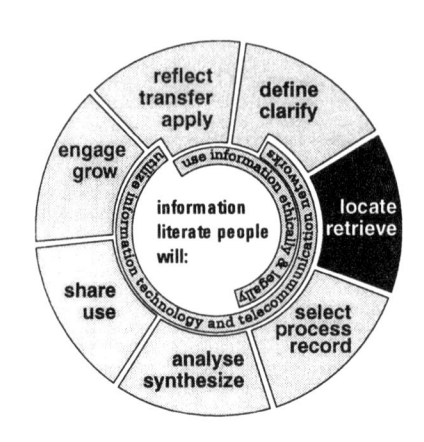

Once students have a clearly defined information need, they are ready to locate and retrieve resources from a variety of sources.

Students can use the school library information centre to

☆ locate picture books, fiction, nonfiction and magazines
☆ locate materials by call number*

They practise appropriate library routines by

☆ observing the rules of conduct
☆ respecting materials
☆ using such available technologies as
    ☆ telephones
    ☆ filmstrip projectors
    ☆ computers
    ☆ televisions and VCRs

Students conduct a search in the card or computer catalogue using*

☆ keywords   ☆ title
☆ author

They check a variety of print and nonprint materials, including

☆ picture books   ☆ CD-ROMs*
☆ nonfiction books   ☆ audio cassettes
☆ pictures   ☆ junior encyclopedias*
☆ video/film   ☆ dictionaries

---

* Younger students will need assistance in doing this.

Discovering Resources

Now you are ready to lead your students in the search for materials that may be useful for their research. Because each student has unique abilities and needs, they require access to a wide variety of resources.

Assist students in visiting their school library information centre to discover

- their helpful teacher-librarian
- friendly volunteers
- exciting displays
- comfortable work areas
- a variety of genres for personal reading
- a variety of resources to meet their learning needs
- how easy it is to borrow materials

Using the Library Information Centre

The reproducible pages will assist students in learning how to locate appropriate sources in their school library information centre and the public library. You and your teacher-librarian can use the activity on page 27 to give your students practice in locating library materials.

Students should discover the power of such technologies as

- filmstrip viewers
- tape players/recorders
- video cameras
- telephones
- fax machines
- computer
    - browsers
    - CD-ROMs
    - modems
    - word processing
    - graphics applications
    - multimedia
    - telecommunications

Using Your School Library

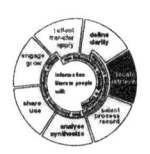

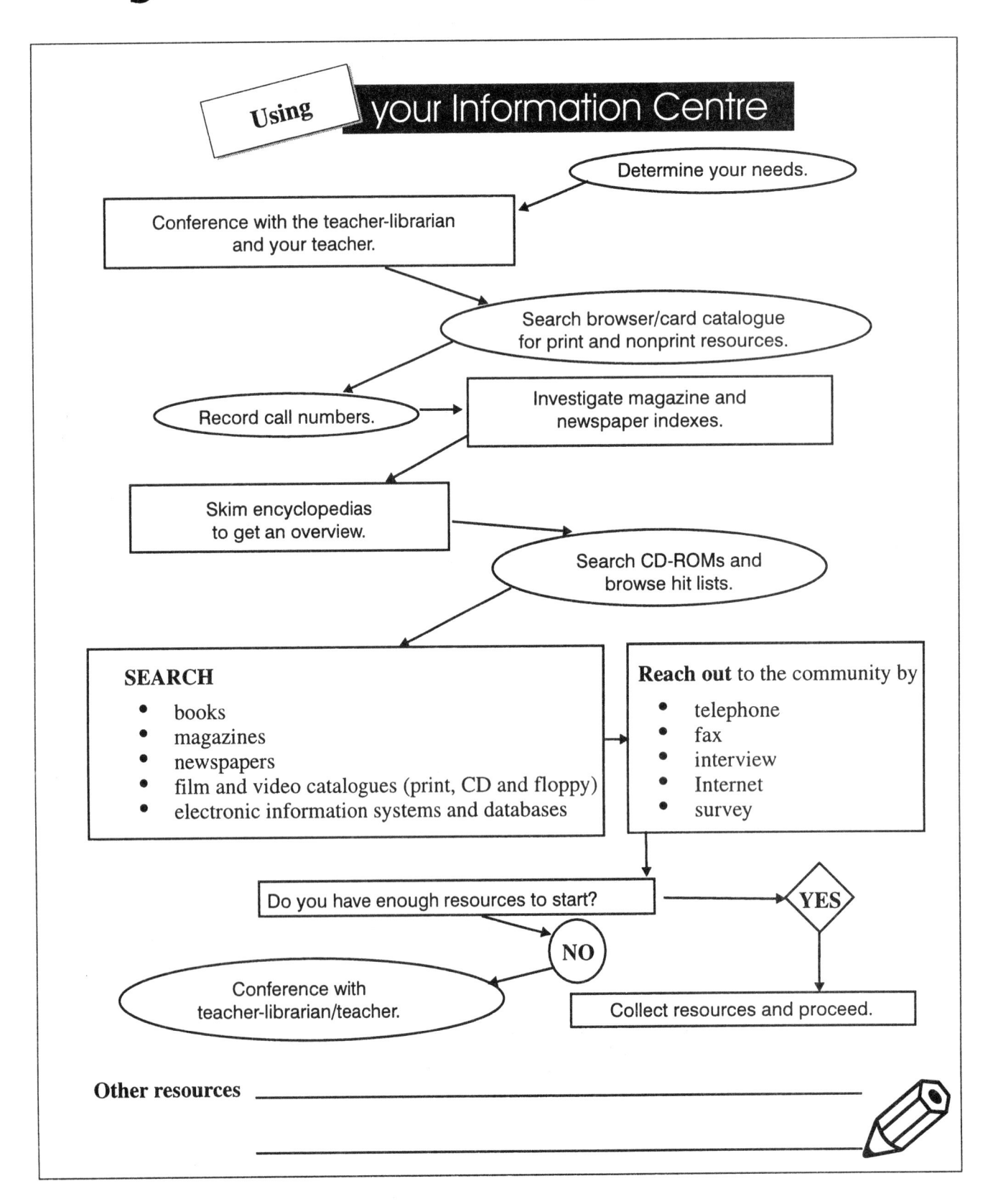

Using your Information Centre

- Determine your needs.
- Conference with the teacher-librarian and your teacher.
- Search browser/card catalogue for print and nonprint resources.
- Record call numbers.
- Investigate magazine and newspaper indexes.
- Skim encyclopedias to get an overview.
- Search CD-ROMs and browse hit lists.

SEARCH
- books
- magazines
- newspapers
- film and video catalogues (print, CD and floppy)
- electronic information systems and databases

Reach out to the community by
- telephone
- fax
- interview
- Internet
- survey

Do you have enough resources to start?

- YES → Collect resources and proceed.
- NO → Conference with teacher-librarian/teacher.

Other resources _____

_____

26

Tip

Record call numbers and locations.

Bookmark Internet sites.

Ready to Search?

Successful Searches depend on keywords.

Search Strategies

1. Select a Keyword.
2. Try the singular or plural form of the keyword. (computer/computers)
3. Try surname first. (Bell, A. Graham)
4. Try words with similar meaning (use a thesaurus). (car/vehicle)
5. Try expanding or narrowing your topic. (cats/felines/Siamese)
6. Use the Boolean features (and/or/without).
7. Check availability.

Boolean Searches FOCUS your hits.

A and B = blue jays AND baseball

A or B = blue jays OR baseball

A and not B = blue jays AND NOT baseball

Locating Materials — Scavenger Hunt

Plan a student Scavenger Hunt with the teacher-librarian. Select fiction and nonfiction titles for students to locate in the library. Use a curriculum topic as the theme. Make index cards as described in the examples below, then have the students locate the items. Include video, CD-ROM, filmstrips, specific articles in magazines . . .

Procedure

- each student receives a card
- students locate the appropriate shelf or item
- peruse materials or exchange card with teacher and search again

Locate picture books by

☆ initial of the author

| M | H | W | B | Z |

☆ spine label

| E Mun | E Wal | E Zol |

☆ spine label and title

| From Far Away / E / Mun | The Tree / E / Wal |

Locate nonfiction by

☆ call number

| 398.2 Dep | 811 O'Hu |

☆ call number and title

| Streganona / 398.2 / Dep | Scarey Poems For Rotten Kids / 811 / O'Hu |

27

Checking the Source

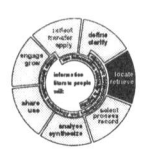

What is being presented?
☆ facts
☆ opinions

Who is presenting it?
☆ expert
☆ special-interest group
☆ government agency
☆
☆

When was it presented?
☆ date it was published or produced
☆ © copyright date

How is it being presented?
☆ table of contents
☆ index
☆ headings and subtitles
☆ visuals
   ☆ pictures
   ☆ charts
   ☆ graphs
   ☆ maps

Is this resource a good choice for my needs?

Why or Why not?

*From *Introducing Insects* by Pamela M. Hickman. Illustrations by Judie Shore. Pembroke Publishers.

Searching

Searching

I searched my library information centre and I discovered ...

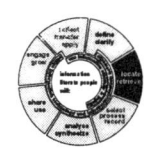

❑ a book about _____ that interested me.

Its title is _____

Its Call Number

❑ a fairy tale I would like to read.

Its title is _____

Its Call Number

❑ a poetry book that looks good.

Its title is _____

Its Call Number

❑ a magazine I might borrow.

Its title is _____

❑ a CD-ROM I want to use.

Its title is _____

❑ a filmstrip/video I would like to see.

Its title is _____

I needed help _____
_____

Name _____

29

I Use My Library Information Centre

My School _____

Teacher-Librarian _____

I can

with help	by myself	
❏	❏	find a storybook
❏	❏	find a fact book
❏	❏	find a magazine
❏	❏	search in the browser/card catalogue
❏	❏	listen to a tape
❏	❏	view a filmstrip
❏	❏	use a CD-ROM
❏	❏	make a picture on the computer
❏	❏	write a story on the computer
❏	❏	make a phone call
❏	❏	send a fax

I want to learn how to _____
_____
_____

Name _____

Trips to My Public Library

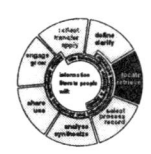

Name _____

Address _____

Telephone _____

Librarian _____

Days and hours the library is open

Monday	Tuesday	Wednesday	Thursday	Friday	Saturday

Date of visit _____

I went with _____

It was a good trip because _____

_____

Date of visit _____

I went with _____

It was a good trip because _____

_____

Date of visit _____

I went with _____

It was a good trip because _____

_____

Interviewing and Conducting Surveys

A powerful way for students to acquire information is by interacting with people. Both interviews and surveys can be very successful — even for younger children — if the experience is carefully structured.

It is often best to generate the interview/survey questions as a group effort. First, invite the students to identify what information the interviewer/surveyor hopes to obtain. List this information as a guide for composing the questions.

The Survey Process

1. As a group, create questions that will elicit the desired information. Record these on a chart as you create them, and later on small cue cards.

2. Decide on an organizer to record the information on. If your students have used organizers often, they will be able to produce one of their own. If not, you will need to guide them through the process of creating one that has the appropriate columns and headings.

3. Invite your students to make predictions about the outcome of the survey and to give reasons for their predictions.

4. Have students work in pairs to practise and then conduct the survey, alternating the roles of questioner and recorder. Each pair should have specific instructions on who to question and suitable days/times to conduct their survey.

5. Ask the pairs of students to tally the results of their survey and to compare them with their predictions.

6. Share the findings from all the pairs and tally the results.

7. Create graphs to display the data visually (line, pie, bar, pictograph).

8. Encourage groups of students to discuss and reflect on the results.
   We discovered ..., It was difficult to ..., I wonder if ...

9. Share the results
   ☆ on the PA announcements
   ☆ in an assembly
   ☆ in a newsletter ...

> Could you please answer a few questions to help us with our school survey?
> Thank you.

> Our class is trying to find out which sports are the most popular in our community. What are the top three sports that you play?

Our Pictograph of Learning Buddy Pets								Totals
fish	🐟	🐟	🐟					3
turtles	🐢	🐢	🐢	🐢	🐢			5
rabbits	🐰							1
birds	🐦	🐦	🐦					3
guinea pigs	🐹	🐹	🐹	🐹	🐹			5
cats	🐱	🐱	🐱	🐱				4
dogs	🐶	🐶						2
no pets	NP	NP	NP	NP	NP	NP		6

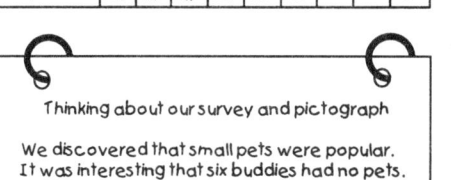

Thinking about our survey and pictograph

We discovered that small pets were popular.
It was interesting that six buddies had no pets.
We are going to ask our buddies to help us discover more about pets.
We wonder if ... ...
Perhaps ... ...

Kinders Can Too

Even kindergarten children can conduct a simple survey to discover the most common pet among their grade four learning buddies. They can participate in all the same activities if they are teacher-led. They will be effective data collectors in years to come.

Successful Surveys

Here's a survey that records the 3 favourite sports that young people play in their community.

Sport Participation Survey

Purpose: To discover and graph student participation in sports.
Criteria: ranking of 3 sports
individual or team sports
gender of participant
age of participant
Target Group: 10 young people in our community
between ages 6 and 13
family or friends

Legend: **I** = individual   **T** = team sport   **M** = male   **F** = female

	1st sport	2nd sport	3rd sport	age	gender
1.	*jogging* **I**	*softball* **T**	*skating* **I**	10	*M*
2.	*swimming* **I**	*cycling* **I**	*tennis* **I**	12	*F*
3.	*gymnastics* **I**	*swimming* **I**	*N.A.*	7	*M*
4.	*basketball* **T**	*skiing* **I**	*rollerblading* **I**	13	
5.	*hockey* **T**	*soccer* **T**	*volleyball*		

ACTION PLAN
- state your purpose
- decide on criteria to be surveyed
- select your target group
- design a neat organizer or questionnaire
- conduct your survey
- thank your participants
- tabulate your results
- analyse your data
- summarize or graph your results

Interviewing

There will be many times when the only way to get the information needed is to do an interview or a survey. Use these tips to guide your students through the process.

Before the Interview
- ✔ get permission from your teacher or parents
- ✔ explain who you are, what information you need and why you need it
- ✔ prepare a list of specific questions
- ✔ get permission if you plan to videotape or audiotape
- ✔ arrange a time and place
- ✔ prepare a list of questions
- ✔ practise with a partner

During the Interview
- ✔ in person, on the Internet or by E-mail, by phone
- ✔ be on time
- ✔ listen actively
- ✔ take accurate notes on an organizer

After the Interview
- ✔ organize your information
- ✔ write your summary
- ✔ send a thank-you note and a copy of your summary to your expert

Connecting to Human Resources

Don't overlook these valuable resources:

authors	illustrators	poets	actors
puppeteers	magicians	musicians	
artists	dancers	parents	
grandparents	students	community experts	
reading buddies	teachers	learning buddies	
scientists	neighbours		

Having guests in your school gives your students an opportunity to apply their social skills and creative talents. They can create invitations, welcome banners, introductions, thank yous…

3

Select, Process and Record Relevant Data

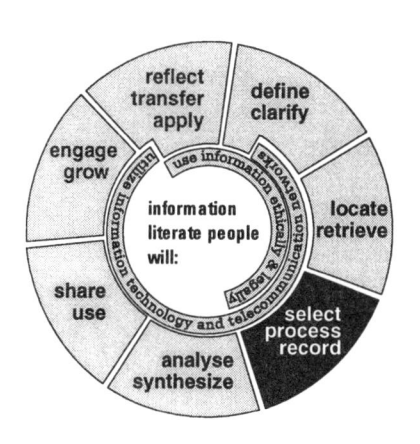

When students have retrieved a few resources, then they are ready to learn how to select, process and record data that is relevant to their needs and interests.

Students can use use criteria for selecting data by

☆ deciding if the data is on topic
☆ evaluating the data for interest
☆ distinguishing fact from fiction
☆ reading text or pictures
☆ making sure to examine a variety of sources

They organize the data they have selected by

☆ using an organizer (provided for them)
☆ arranging the data in subtopics on the organizer
☆ recording data in dot-jot notes, charts or sketches
☆ keeping their organizers, pictures, and so on in a research folder

Students develop an awareness of the ethical and legal use of information by

☆ ensuring that all their work is original (excepting properly acknowledged quotes, examples, etc.)
☆ recording the sources of their data*

They select and employ appropriate tools to record and organize information, including

☆ pencils, paper
☆ organizer
☆ tape recorder
☆ word processor*

---

* Younger students will need assistance in doing this.

Selecting Data

Now you are ready to guide your students in selecting the data for a project. Their success in selecting data depends on

- ☆ the resources they locate
- ☆ their reading skills
- ☆ their viewing skills
- ☆ their listening skills
- ☆ their ability to interpret charts, maps, graphs

You can use the following reproducible pages in assisting students in developing and practising these essential literacy skills.

Reading Pictures

Photographs and illustrations contain a wealth of information that can be readily accessed by all students — readers, nonreaders, ESL, etc. Learning how to read pictures greatly enhances the information accessing process.

Why Learners Read Pictures

- ☆ the learner is a nonreader
- ☆ the written text is too difficult
- ☆ as an exploration of a topic
- ☆ to gather facts
- ☆ to improve confidence and self-esteem
- ☆ to establish related vocabulary
- ☆ to discover the need for new vocabulary

Teaching Children to Read Pictures

First ask them to look at the whole picture. Guide your students using a series of prompts like the following to help them discover the "messages" in a picture.

Invite students to look for:

Who and **What**

- ☆ are the largest things or people?
- ☆ people or things are in the centre of the picture?

Where

Are there clues to the messages in the picture?

☆ trees
☆ buildings
☆ equipment, vehicles
☆ animals, plants
☆ furniture
☆

When

☆ the time of day
☆ the season
☆ whether it's set in the past, present, future

Action

☆ What is happening?
☆ What might have happened before the scene in the picture?
☆ What might happen next?
☆

Colour

Is the picture

☆ black-and-white or in colour?
☆ bright or dull?
☆ dark or light?
☆

Now encourage the students to look at the picture again. This time they are to discover little things, details.

Tip
Prompts like the following will help students make connections between the data they have gathered and their personal experiences.
- Have you ever …?
- Would you like …?
- Can you imagine …?
- What do you think about …?
- How do you feel …?

Listening

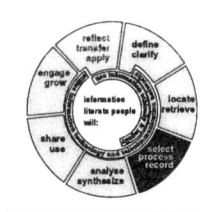

It is important for you to become a good listener.

A good listener is an active listener.

Did you know you spend 55 percent of your school day listening?

Active Listeners

STOP all other activities.

LOOK directly at the speaker.

LISTEN and reflect.

REACT
Identify the important points.
Make mental pictures.
Record in point form.
Make sketches.
Make connections.

Here's where I can gain information by listening
☆
☆
☆
☆

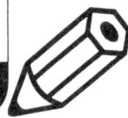

Make connections between what you hear and what you already know.

MAXIMUM
TALKING
125
THINKING
400
WORDS/MINUTE

Viewing

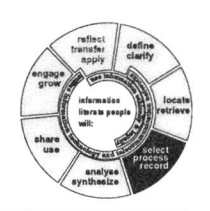

Ask yourself:

Am I getting **facts**, **opinions** or **both**?

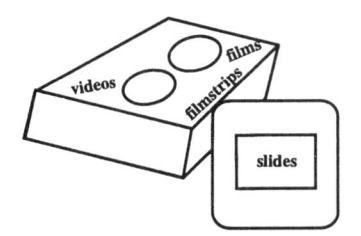

Use Audio-Visuals & Discover

- ✔ an entertaining way to review
- ✔ more realistic detail
- ✔ lots of information in a short time
- ✔ new connections for your ideas
- ✔ a springboard for new ideas
- ✔ an active way to learn
- ✔ a valuable source of background information

Always be an active viewer.

Use audio-visual resources as you use print resources.

Independent Viewing

Pay attention to
- ✔ images
- ✔ words and music
- ✔ filming techniques

VIEW

First	▲	for an overview of the main topic
Second	▲	for subtopics
Again	▲	for specific information
and	▲	fast forward, start, stop, pause
Again	▲	note what you need

Reading

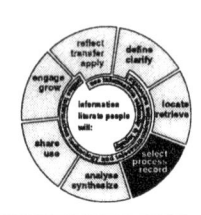

Why are you reading?
- collect information
- general information
- fact finding
- fun
- relaxation

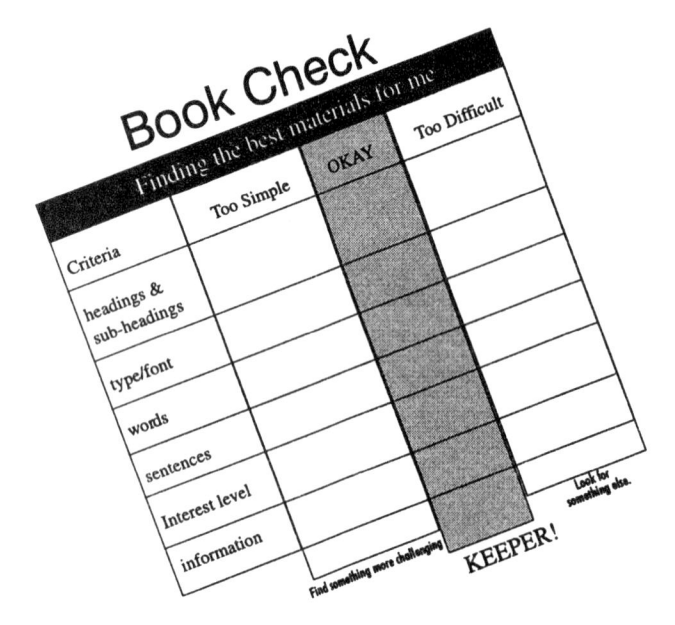

Skim for an overview by looking at the title, first paragraph, headings or first sentences of each paragraph, illustrations and last paragraph.

Scan for a specific piece of information such as a telephone number or a fact from a long list.

The Reading Mystery

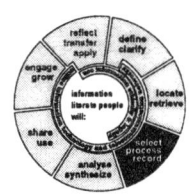

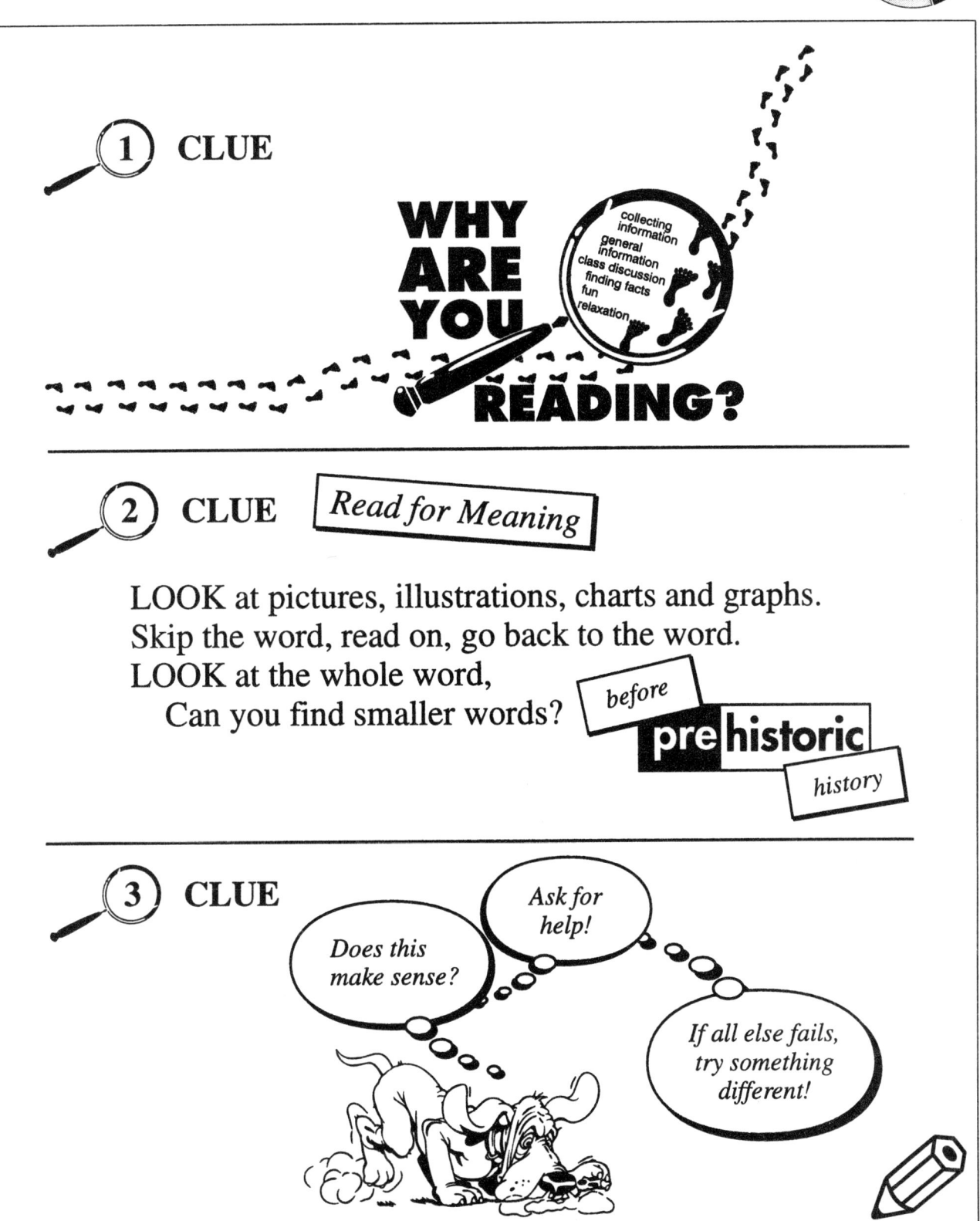

1 CLUE

WHY ARE YOU READING?

- collecting information
- general information
- class discussion
- finding facts
- fun
- relaxation

2 CLUE — Read for Meaning

LOOK at pictures, illustrations, charts and graphs.
Skip the word, read on, go back to the word.
LOOK at the whole word,
   Can you find smaller words?

before • pre**historic** • history

3 CLUE

Does this make sense?

Ask for help!

If all else fails, try something different!

41

Collecting Information

Now students will apply skills in reading, writing, listening, and viewing to begin collecting information.

In becoming information literate, students need to be aware of the importance of investigating a number of different sources. They must develop an awareness that authors and producers bring their own interpretations and perspective to a work. By gathering data from a variety of sources and media, students will gain a balanced view of a topic. Even very young researchers can see the improvement that results from using multiple sources.

You can model this concept. For example:

Topic: Grizzly Bears

Day 1 Introduce the topic grizzly bears.

Use the **KNL** model:

> What do you **K**now about grizzly bears?
> What do you **N**eed to find out about them?
> Where can you **L**earn about grizzly bears?

View a video about grizzlies.

Collaboratively record all the facts the class discovered in the video.

Day 2 Read a nonfiction book about grizzlies aloud to the class.

Collaboratively recall and record facts the students gleaned from the book.

This is an excellent time to reinforce the skill of reading pictures for information.

Day 3 Compare "grizzly facts" gathered from the video with those from the book. Look for similarities and differences as well as discrepancies in the data.

If there are discrepancies or a need to confirm facts, ask your students what they think they should do next …

Introduce more sources.

Show your students the comparison by using a Venn diagram.

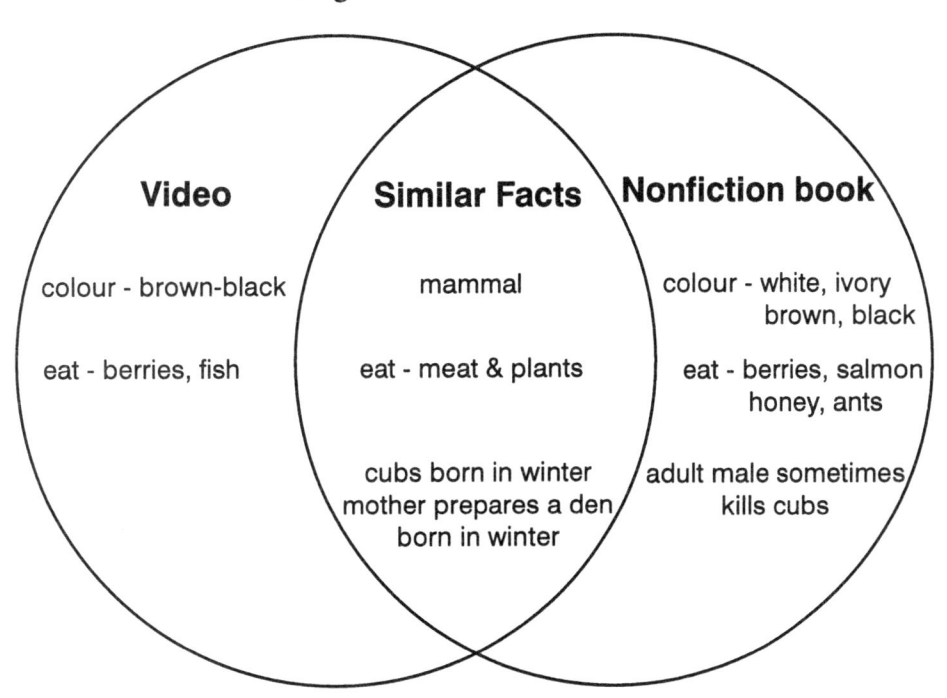

Video
- colour - brown-black
- eat - berries, fish

Similar Facts
- mammal
- eat - meat & plants
- cubs born in winter
- mother prepares a den
- born in winter

Nonfiction book
- colour - white, ivory, brown, black
- eat - berries, salmon, honey, ants
- adult male sometimes kills cubs

> **TIP**
>
> Overlap two Hula-Hoops to create a Venn diagram. Cut out facts so that students can place them inside different sections to sort and classify. This demonstration will help students acquire a concrete understanding of the sorting and classifying process.

In this example, students noticed a discrepancy about the colour of the grizzly bear. Only one source mentioned that the adult male sometimes kills cubs. So that fact would be double-checked in another source to confirm its validity.

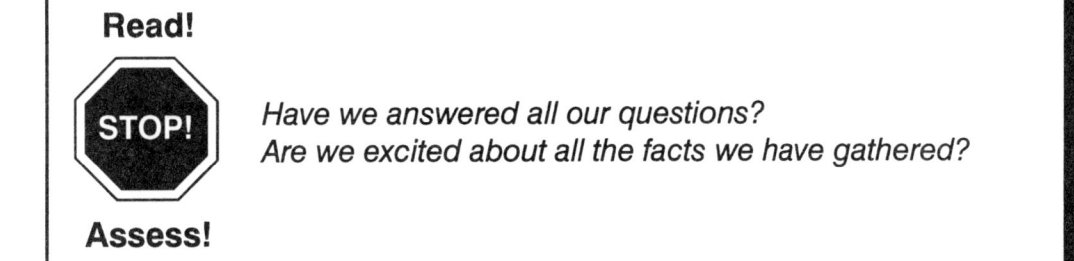

Read!
STOP!
Assess!

Have we answered all our questions?
Are we excited about all the facts we have gathered?

Fact and Fiction

Young researchers also need to be able to differentiate between fact and fiction. You can assist them in developing this skill by using a process similar to the one for comparing facts from different sources (pages 42 to 43).

First, model the process as a class lesson to introduce the skills to your students. Next, have them practise the skills, working in groups.

Read a fiction storybook about a grizzly bear. Record facts about a grizzly bear.

Read a nonfiction book about grizzly bears.

Record facts about the bear. Compare facts on an organizer.

Look for similarities and differences.

Follow with lots of discussion.

☆ Why are there differences?
☆ Are there any facts in fiction books?
☆ Where do authors get facts?
☆ Compare illustrations.

Topic: Grizzly Bears		
Fiction		**Nonfiction**
Title: Fun in the Woods		**Title:** Bears of the Wild
- forest - in a cottage - furniture	Habitat	- forest - mother makes a den - lines den with grass, ferns, leaves
- pizza, cupcakes, pop, honey, strawberries	Food	- salmon, honey berries, ants
- play with balls - sing songs	Young	- cubs born in winter - stay close to mother for 2 years

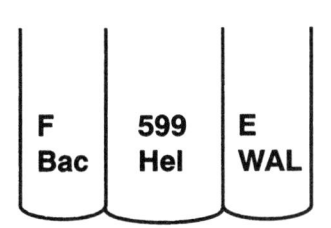

Discuss and chart similarities and differences in the physical appearances of fiction and nonfiction books.

Examine

- ☆ call number
- ☆ size
- ☆ cover illustrations
- ☆ organization: chapters, table of contents, index …

Explain

- ☆ Fiction entertains.
- ☆ Nonfiction informs.

Recording Data

Now your students are ready to record the data they have selected. They should record their data on an organizer as they collect it, using dot-jot notes and sketches — not sentences.

Students should sort their data into subtopics now.

This process will help them to think about information and analyse it.

It will save them lots of time.

They won't be wasting time recording useless information.

All the information will be useful.

> **Model this process for your class.**

On the next page, you will find information to help model for students how to select and record information, using dot-jot notes.

Organizers on pages 47 to 51 will assist your students in analysing the data they have discovered.

After students have had numerous experiences using a variety of teacher-designed organizers, they will be ready to begin creating their own.

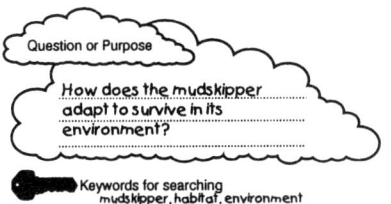

Dot-Jot Notes

☆ begin each line with a point or nugget
☆ important words only
☆ no punctuation
☆ no sentences
☆ brief

First ...

read,

view or

listen, to get an overall impression.

Is there information you need?

Next ...

read,

view or

listen, to identify words or phrases to record.

Then ...

dot-jot onto your organizer,

sketch onto your organizer.

If you have a printout from a CD-ROM, use a highlighter to identify words and phrases. Then ... dot-jot!

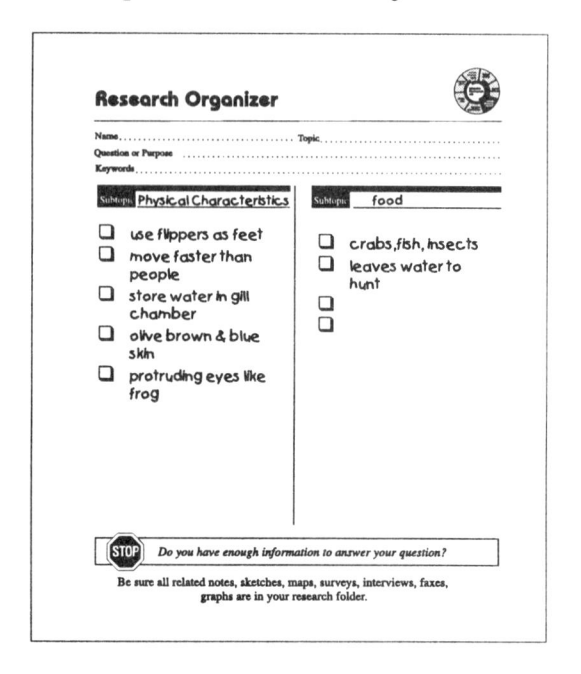

Mudskipper

This unusual fish sometimes leaves the water to hunt for crabs, fish and insects. When out of water the mudskipper uses its flippers as feet. Some mudskippers can move faster than a person.

The mudskipper survives out of water by carrying its own water supply. It stores water in sacs, called gill chambers, inside its body. The mudskipper's olive brown and blue skin provides excellent camouflage. Its protruding, mobile eyes give it a frog like appearance.

Research Organizer

Name.......................... Topic..........................
Question or Purpose ....
Keywords ....

Subtopic: Physical Characteristics
☐ use flippers as feet
☐ move faster than people
☐ store water in gill chamber
☐ olive brown & blue skin
☐ protruding eyes like frog

Subtopic: food
☐ crabs, fish, insects
☐ leaves water to hunt
☐
☐

STOP Do you have enough information to answer your question?
Be sure all related notes, sketches, maps, surveys, interviews, faxes, graphs are in your research folder.

Survival

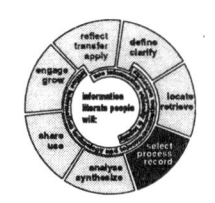

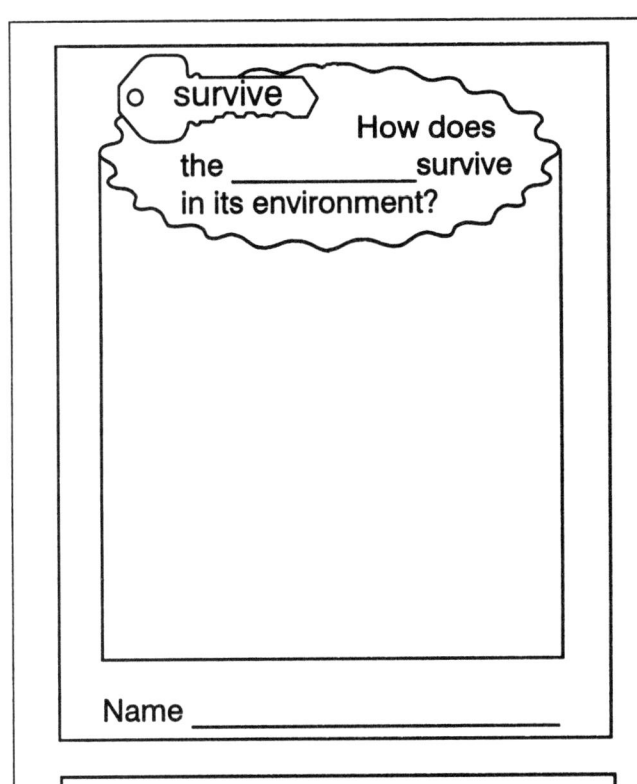

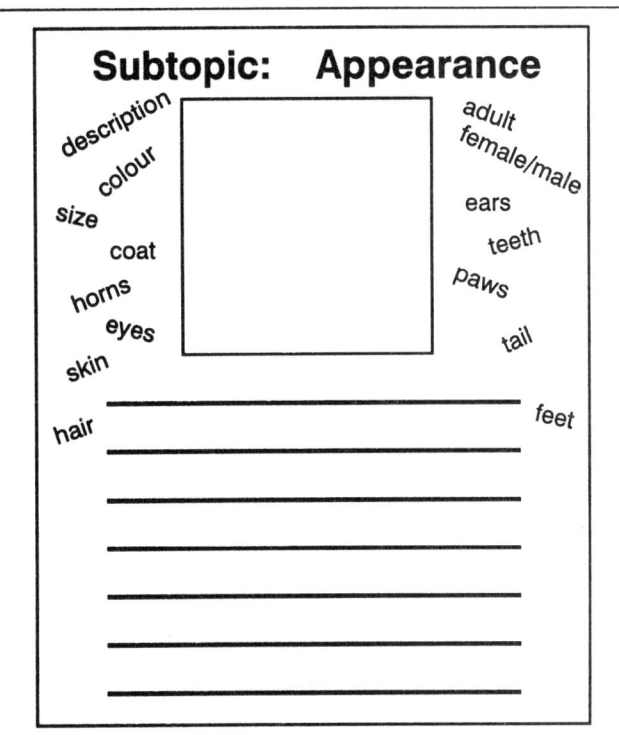

How does the _____ survive in its environment?

survive

Name _____

Subtopic: Appearance

description
colour
size
coat
horns
eyes
skin
hair

adult
female/male
ears
teeth
paws
tail
feet

_____
_____
_____
_____
_____
_____

Subtopic: Habitat

- What does it use as its home?
- How is it designed?
- Where is it located?

where does it live?
- forest
- jungle
- marsh

territory space
natural environment
What materials is the home made from?

shelter

_____
_____
_____
_____

Subtopic: Food

What does the adult eat?
diet
feeding
prey

Does it hunt?
What do the young eat?

_____
_____
_____
_____
_____
_____

Survival

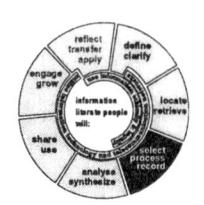

Subtopic: Family Life

babies, young, birth, protection, life cycle, mating, lifespan, relatives

_____
_____
_____
_____
_____
_____

Subtopic: Enemies

Natural Enemies
- adults
- young
predators, overhunting, pollution, sickness

_____
_____
_____
_____
_____
_____

Subtopic: Survival Skills

Special Skills
• sight
• speed
• hearing
• senses
teeth, claws, signals, structure, protection

_____
_____
_____
_____
_____
_____

My Learning

☐ I discovered a lot of good information about the _____
☐ I organized my discoveries
☐ I used dot jots & sketches
☐ I recorded my sources

I think that the _____ *survives* in its environment because _____
_____
_____

Now I want to share my learning by _____
_____

48

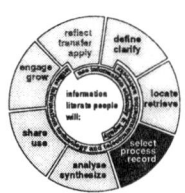

I wonder

I wonder about _____
_____

Name _____

I want to know
🔑 where _____
I discovered _____
- _____
- _____
- _____
- _____
- _____
- _____
- _____

I would like to know
🔑 when _____
I discovered _____
- _____
- _____
- _____
- _____
- _____
- _____
- _____

I would like to know
🔑 why _____
I discovered _____
- _____
- _____
- _____
- _____
- _____
- _____
- _____

I wonder

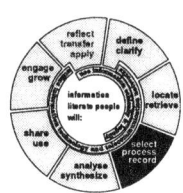

I would like to know
- what _____
- I discovered _____
  - _____
  - _____
  - _____
  - _____
  - _____

I want to know
- how _____
- I discovered _____
  - _____
  - _____
  - _____
  - _____
  - _____

I would like to know
- who _____
- I discovered _____
  - _____
  - _____
  - _____
  - _____
  - _____

My Learning

☐ I discovered a lot of good information about _____

☐ I organized my discoveries.
☐ I used dot-jots & sketches.
☐ I recorded my sources.

I think that the _____
_____
_____
_____

Now I want to share my learning by _____
_____

Use Your Learning Tools to Make Discoveries

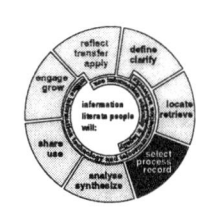

👁 seeing	👂 hearing	smelling 👃
👄 tasting	✋ feeling	💭 thinking

I am becoming a scientific discovery learner.

I wonder about _____

I see _____
I hear _____
I feel _____
I smell _____
I taste _____
I discovered _____
_____
My Name is _____

You will enjoy using flip books to record your discoveries.

? ? I wonder about ?
? oviparous animals. ?
? ? ? ? ? ? ?

I discovered ...
I discovered ...
I discovered ...

51

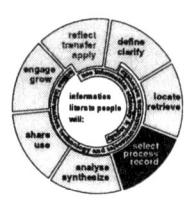

Making Discoveries

I wonder ...

Perhaps ....

I tried ...

A picture of what happened

I discovered ...

Now I need to know

My Family

People in my family ...	My home ...
Working ...	Playing
Food ...	Favourite times ...

Research Topic

I want to know	My source is
	❑ Book ❑ Filmstrip ❑ CD ROM ❑ Video/Film

I discovered great things!

①	②
③	④

My Research

❑ Film   ❑ Video   ❑ Book   ❑ CD ROM

Topic:
I want to know

I watched / read / listened to

I discovered

52

Recording Sources

Assist your students in using the worksheet on the next page to record the sources of their information. Keeping track of their sources will help students begin to develop an awareness of the ethical and legal use of copyright materials.

Student Self-Assessment

Students can use a worksheet like the one below to assess their learning progress at this stage in the research process. If they answer No to any of the questions on the assessment sheet, they will benefit from a conference with the teacher or teacher-librarian. Students may need to revisit some of the resources or locate additional materials.

Topic．．

	YES	NO
Have I found rich information?	❑	❑
Have I found enough information to answer my question?	❑	❑
Have I used a variety of resources?	❑	❑

Is my information	fact? ❑
	opinion? ❑
	both? ❑

	YES	NO
Do I have information from different points of view?	❑	❑
Do I have conflicting information	❑	❑
Have I summarized my new discoveries?	❑	❑
Have I connected similar ideas?	❑	❑
Have I thought about how my learning will affect me and others today and in the future?	❑	❑
Have I made a plan for sharing or using my discoveries?	❑	❑

IF THE ANSWER TO ANY OF THESE QUESTIONS IS NO, CONFERENCE WITH YOUR TEACHER OR TEACHER-LIBRARIAN.

Name．．．

Sources I Have Used

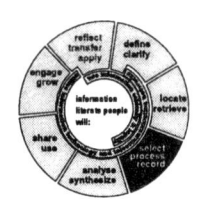

People	☐ my teacher ☐ my librarian ☐ ☐ ☐ ☐
Books	☐ ☐ ☐
Film/Video/ Filmstrips	☐ ☐ ☐
Computer	☐ ☐ ☐
Picture/Magazine/ Poster	☐ ☐ ☐

4

Analyse and Synthesize Information

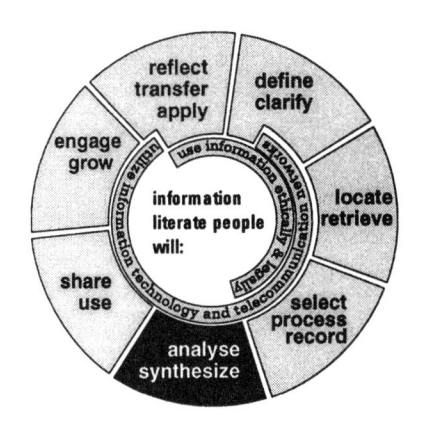

Now students need to learn how to analyse and synthesize the information they have acquired.

Students compare facts from different sources by

☆ finding connections between similar ideas
☆ discovering conflicting data
☆ looking for similarities and differences in data

They draw conclusions by

☆ discovering relationships
☆ determining a point of view
☆ answering the inquiry questions

Students ensure that their information needs have been met by

☆ using self- and peer evaluation
☆ conferencing with
　☆ teacher
　☆ teacher-librarian
　☆ learning buddy

Intellectual Access to Information

The students have made some interesting discoveries.

Their data have been gathered and recorded on organizers.

Now they must progress beyond the stage of physical access to data. They need opportunities to manipulate, reorganize, regroup, to analyse data so that they can see connections and make relationships.

When they use organizers to sort their data into subtopics, students are beginning to analyse. Students analyse when they

- ☆ categorize
- ☆ classify
- ☆ contrast
- ☆ compare
- ☆ predict
- ☆ survey

These experiences afford them intellectual access to information. Only when they have analysed information can they see the connections and possibilities necessary to begin synthesis.

Synthesis

Synthesis is taking all the parts, making personal use of them and putting them back together in a new, meaningful way. It is creating personal knowledge.

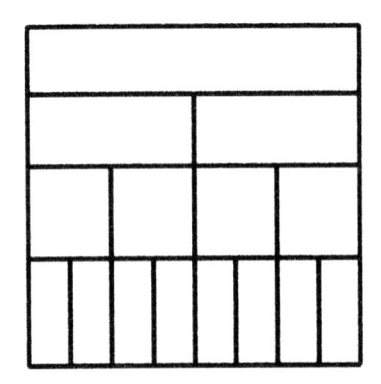

When students synthesize they

- ☆ write
- ☆ invent
- ☆ create
- ☆ compose
- ☆ plan
- ☆ imagine
- ☆

See Share Your Talents, page 72.

Tri-Venn Diagram

Tree Diagram

Practising Analysis and Synthesis

You can give your students lots of practice in analysing and synthesizing by asking them to respond to events and stories with such reflections as

Compared to …

Suppose …

Imagine …

What if …

I wonder …

The following reproducible page will help students stretch their thinking.

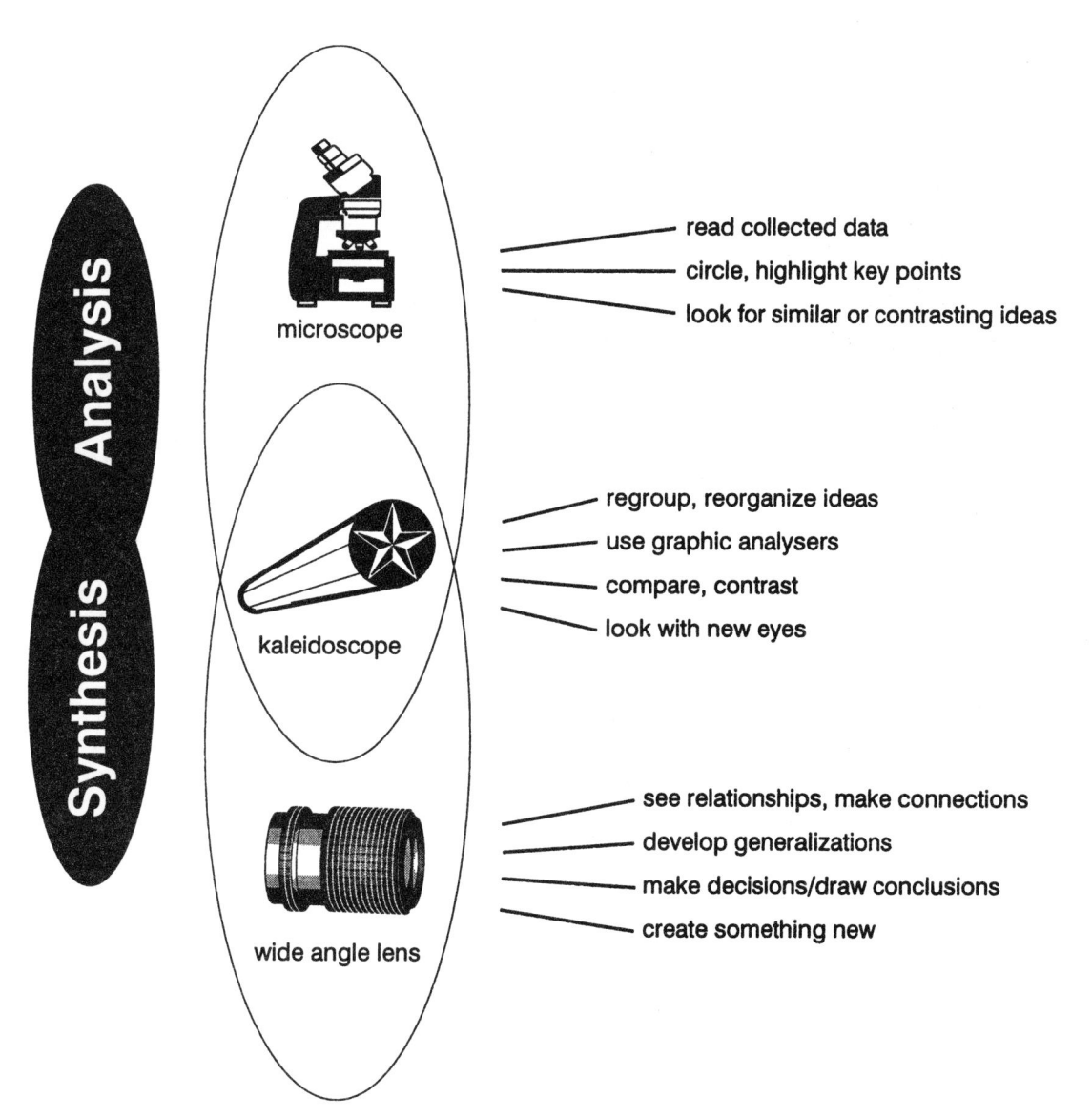

Analysis

microscope
- read collected data
- circle, highlight key points
- look for similar or contrasting ideas

Synthesis

kaleidoscope
- regroup, reorganize ideas
- use graphic analysers
- compare, contrast
- look with new eyes

wide angle lens
- see relationships, make connections
- develop generalizations
- make decisions/draw conclusions
- create something new

57

Stretch Your Thinking by ...

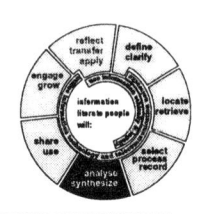

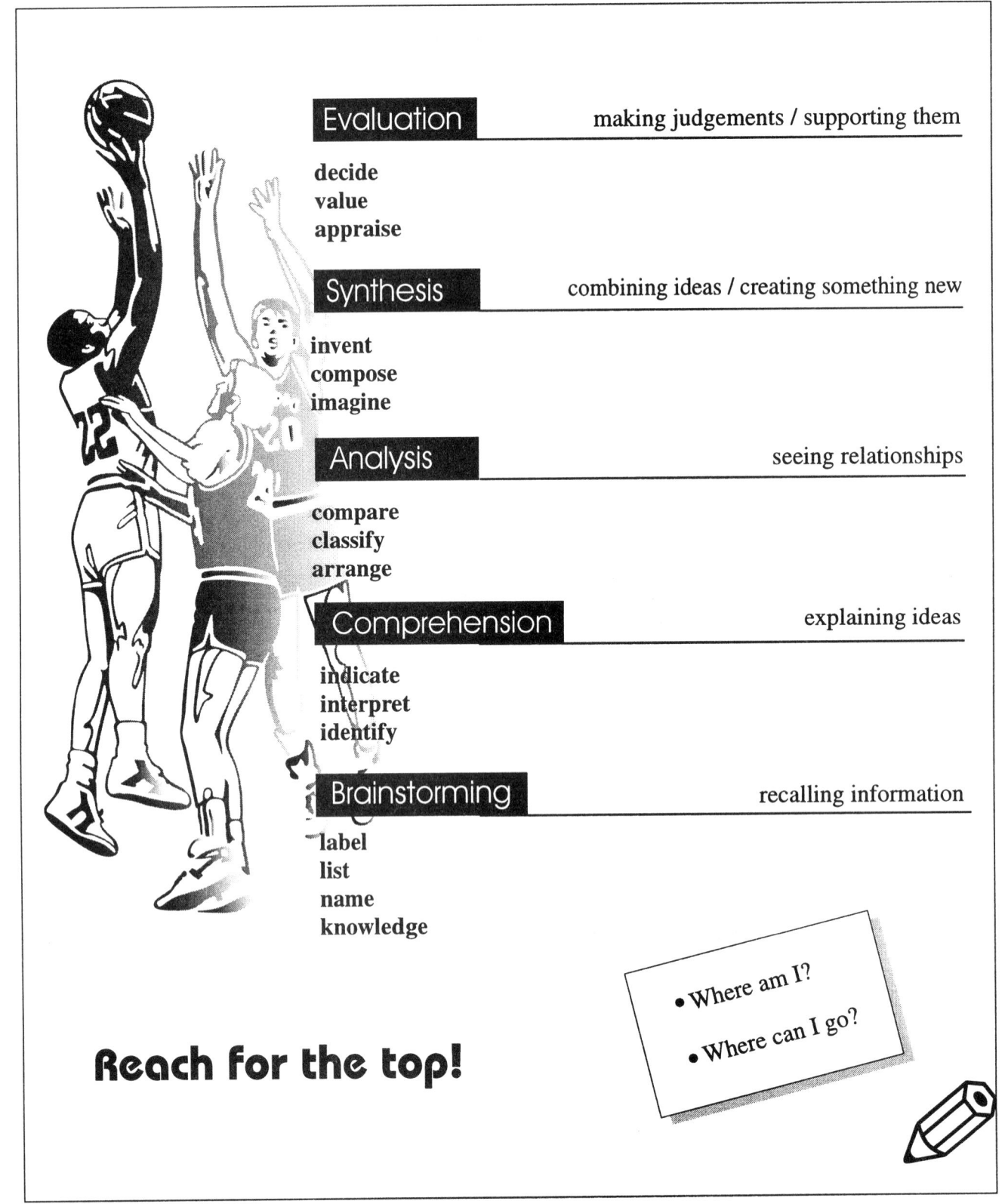

Evaluation
making judgements / supporting them

decide
value
appraise

Synthesis
combining ideas / creating something new

invent
compose
imagine

Analysis
seeing relationships

compare
classify
arrange

Comprehension
explaining ideas

indicate
interpret
identify

Brainstorming
recalling information

label
list
name
knowledge

Reach for the top!

- Where am I?
- Where can I go?

Using Graphic Organizers to Develop Thinking Skills

Using graphic organizers will help students develop their thinking skills. The **T chart** is a powerful organizer. Encourage your students to design their own T chart organizers, like the ones below.

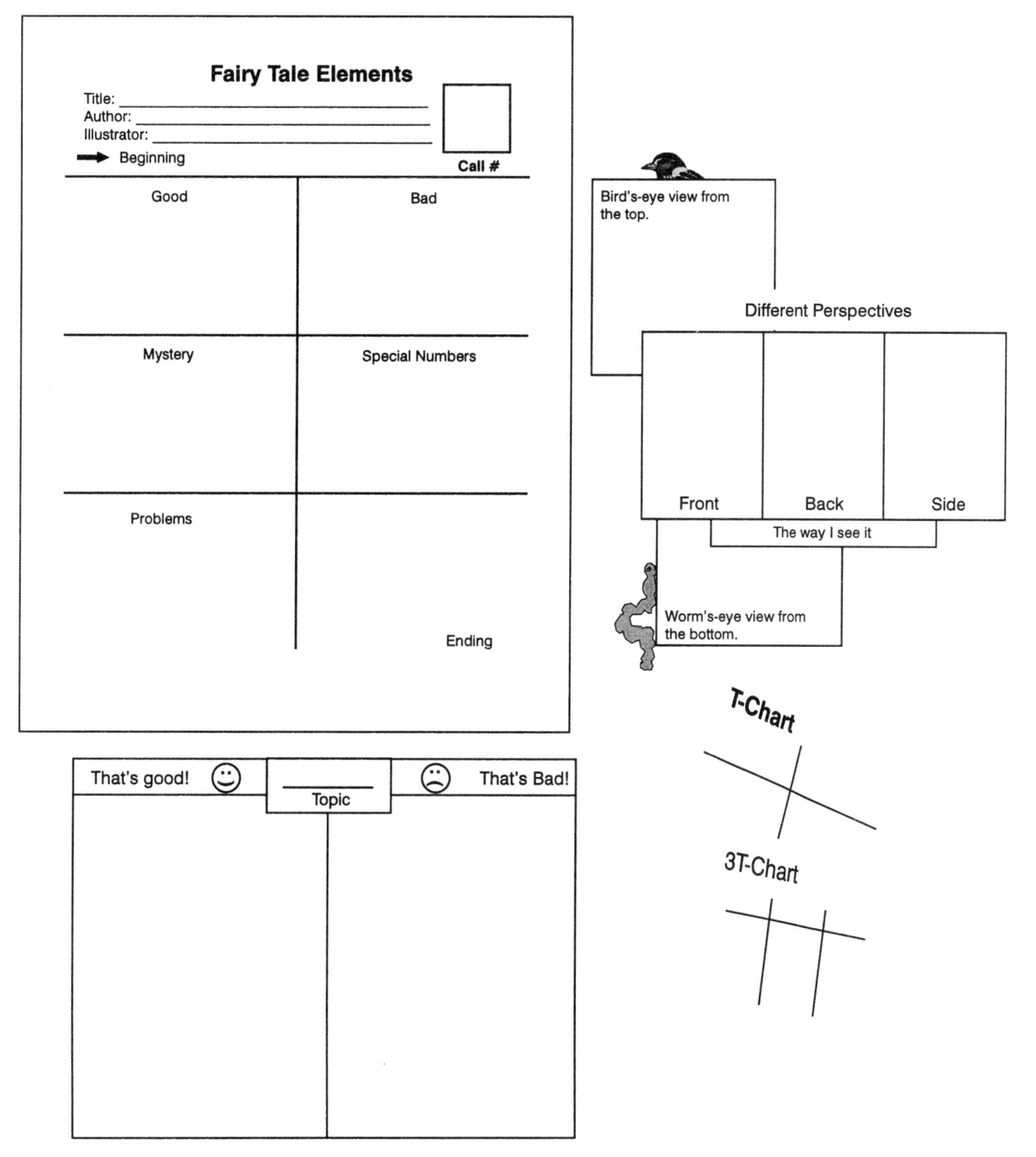

Fairy Tale Elements

Title: _____
Author: _____
Illustrator: _____

→ Beginning   Call #

Good	Bad
Mystery	Special Numbers
Problems	
	Ending

Different Perspectives

Bird's-eye view from the top.

Front	Back	Side

The way I see it

Worm's-eye view from the bottom.

T-Chart

3T-Chart

That's good! ☺   Topic   ☹ That's Bad!

Focus Words

You can reinforce the use of **focus** words by highlighting them on student worksheets.

Influence — How does the changing weather influence what I wear?

Wind	Rain	Heat	Cold

changes ___Trees___ Name ___Assad___

Spring	Summer	Fall	Winter

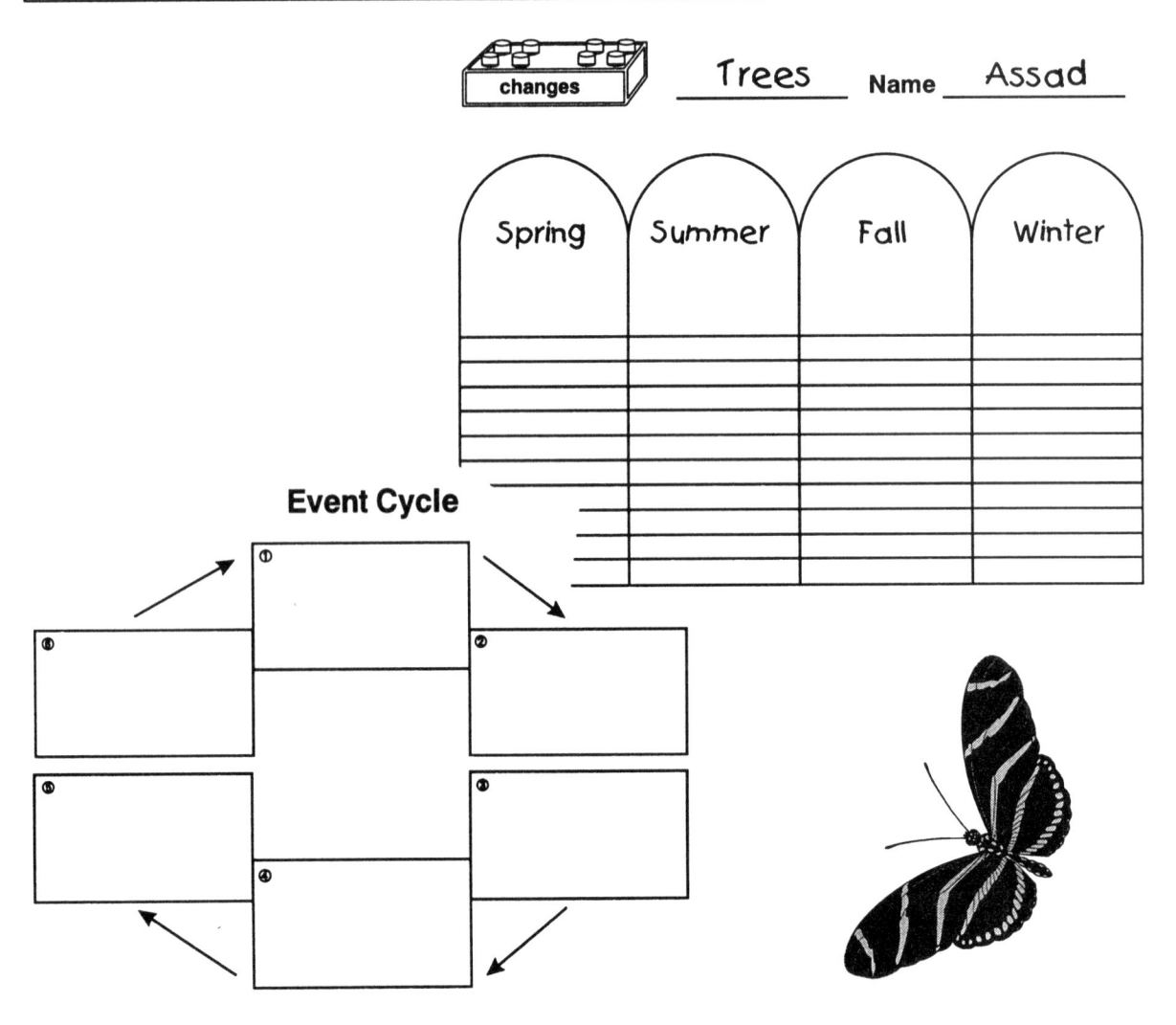

Event Cycle

Higher-Level Thinking Skills

These organizers provide students experiences with higher-level thinking skills.

☆ comparing
☆ evaluating
☆ predicting
☆ analysing
☆ synthesizing
☆

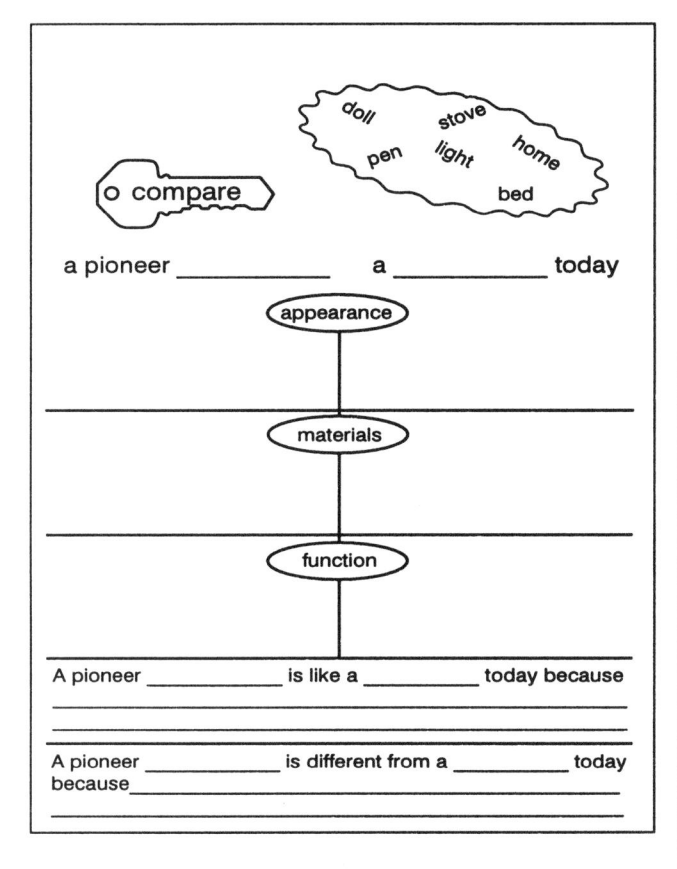

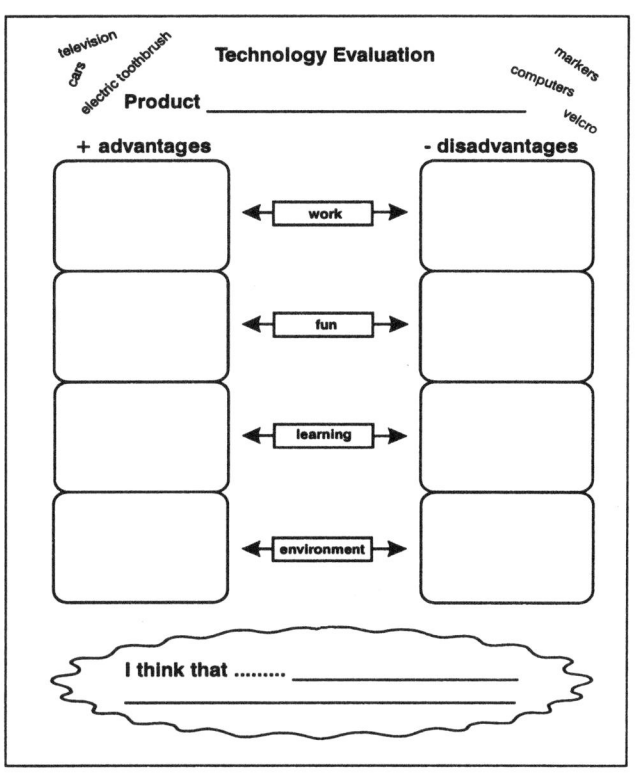

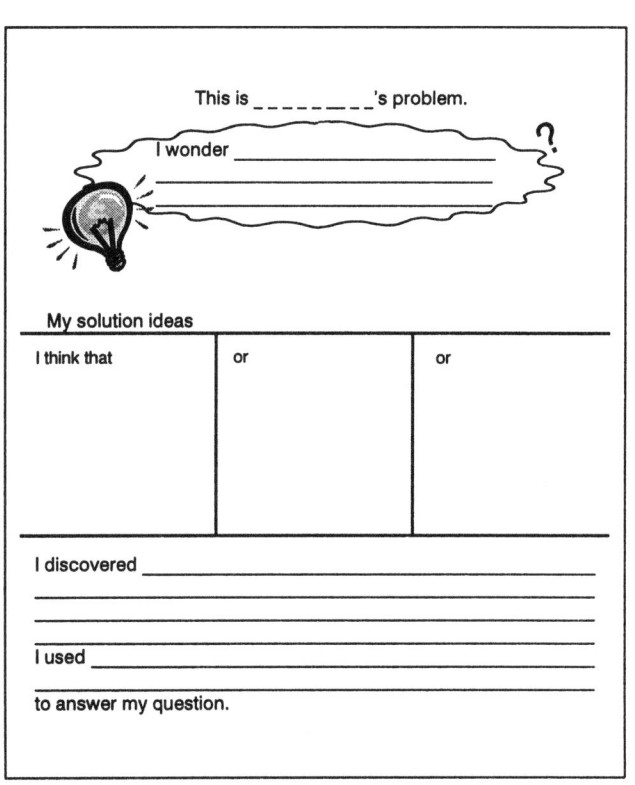

Technology Evaluation

television, cars, electric toothbrush, markers, computers, velcro

Product _____

+ advantages ← work → - disadvantages

← fun →

← learning →

← environment →

I think that .... _____

---

o compare

doll, stove, pen, light, home, bed

a pioneer _____ a _____ today

- appearance
- materials
- function

A pioneer _____ is like a _____ today because _____

A pioneer _____ is different from a _____ today because _____

This is _ _ _ _ _ _ _'s problem.

I wonder _____

My solution ideas

I think that	or	or

I discovered _____

I used _____

to answer my question.

Series Line

Series Line or Time Lines

These organizers visualize a series of events. They can chart events in a story, novel or film.

Try creating two series or time lines to discover the relationships during a period in history.

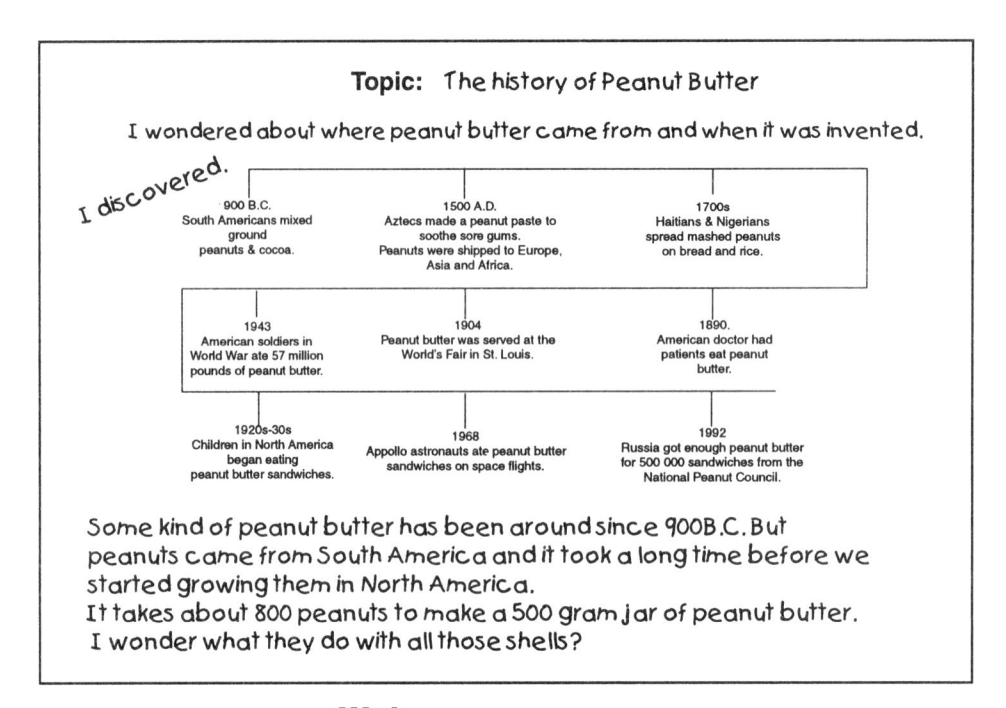

Topic: The history of Peanut Butter

I wondered about where peanut butter came from and when it was invented.

I discovered.

900 B.C.	1500 A.D.	1700s
South Americans mixed ground peanuts & cocoa.	Aztecs made a peanut paste to soothe sore gums. Peanuts were shipped to Europe, Asia and Africa.	Haitians & Nigerians spread mashed peanuts on bread and rice.
1943	1904	1890.
American soldiers in World War ate 57 million pounds of peanut butter.	Peanut butter was served at the World's Fair in St. Louis.	American doctor had patients eat peanut butter.
1920s-30s	1968	1992
Children in North America began eating peanut butter sandwiches.	Appollo astronauts ate peanut butter sandwiches on space flights.	Russia got enough peanut butter for 500 000 sandwiches from the National Peanut Council.

Some kind of peanut butter has been around since 900 B.C. But peanuts came from South America and it took a long time before we started growing them in North America.
It takes about 800 peanuts to make a 500 gram jar of peanut butter.
I wonder what they do with all those shells?

Webs

Web Diagram

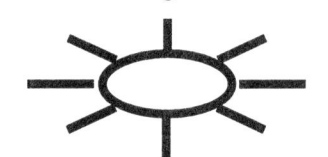

Webs show relationship among ideas.

They break a big idea into progressively smaller parts. Learners can cluster similar ideas together on a web.

Webs are excellent graphic tools for recording brainstorming ideas.

They effectively organize a lot of data.

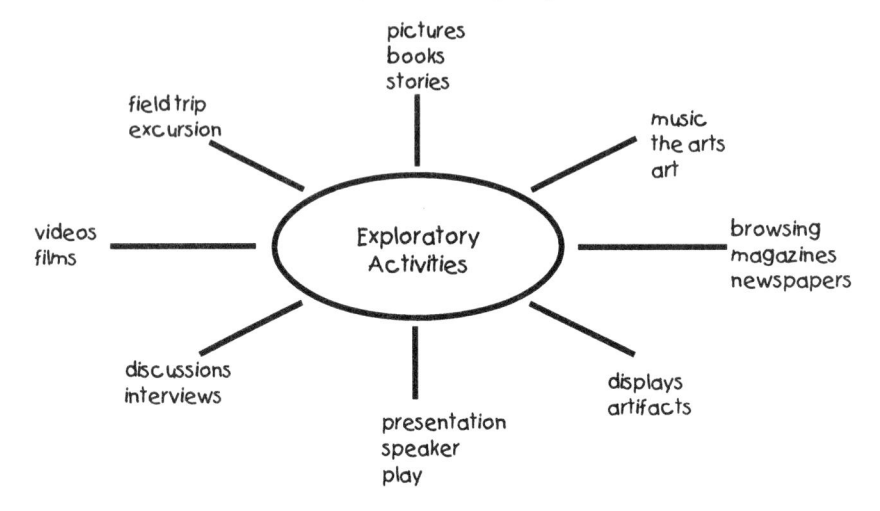

Exploratory Activities
- pictures books stories
- field trip excursion
- music the arts art
- videos films
- browsing magazines newspapers
- discussions interviews
- presentation speaker play
- displays artifacts

Tri-Venn Diagram

Venn Diagrams

These organizers allow students to examine details and make comparisons. Venn diagrams organize similarities and differences.

Frogs Toads Toads Frogs What's the Difference?

Frogs
- teeth
- smooth wet skin
- long hind legs
- long leaps
- eggs in a clump of jelly
- eggs float on water

Both (center)
- mate in wetlands
- lay eggs in wetlands
- hibernate in winter
- cold blooded
- same shape
- same size
- bulging eyes
- sing in evening
- green or brown

Toads
- no teeth
- rough dry skin
- shorter hind legs
- shorter leaps
- eggs in a string of jelly
- eggs around plants under water

I think I could tell which was which by looking at the skin and watching them jump. I wouldn't test to see whether or not they have teeth.

3T-Chart

T Charts

T charts can be used to collect and organize data. They break down ideas.

Topic: Wetlands

That's Good ☺	That's Bad ☹
excellent homes for frogs, toads, birds, moose...	no good for building houses or cottages
mosquitoes are food for dragonflies and bats	mosquitoes breed in stagnant water and bite people
dead trees are homes for insects	trees fall down and die
insects are food for birds	
soft wood crumbles into mulch	birds and animals make holes in dead trees and the wood gets soft
mulch makes new soil for plants to grow in	
cattails and bulrushes soak up harmful chemicals	purple loosestrife grows

I think that we should leave the wetlands the way nature made them because they are a whole ecosystem. Plants and creatures in wetlands depend on each other.

Cross-Classification Chart

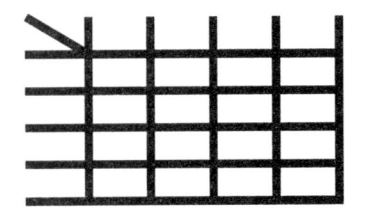

Cross-Classification Charts

These organizers sort facts and similarities. Students can use cross-classification charts to evaluate and classify data. They are an effective tool for making decisions.

Category Breakfast Favourites Rank 0-5	Features Friends								Total
Cold Cereal	1	5	1	4	3	4	5	4	(27)
Hot Cereal	0	4	0	1	0	0	1	2	(8)
Waffles	5	1	2	3	5	2	3	0	(21)
Pancakes	4	2	3	2	4	1	2	1	(19)
Eggs (any style)	2	0	5	0	1	3	0	3	(14)
Toast & spread	3	3	4	5	2	5	4	5	(31)

Reflection
I conclude that toast & spread and cold cereals are the favourite breakfasts of my friends.
I was surprised that hot cereals scored so low.
I wonder what kids in other parts of the world like to eat for breakfast. How could I find out?

Tree Diagram

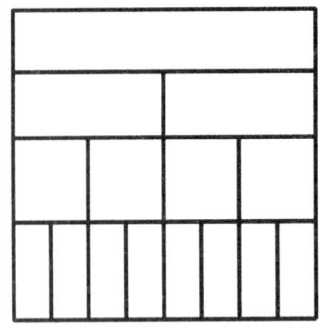

Tree Diagrams

Tree diagrams also break down ideas into progressively smaller parts. They demonstrate an order or ranking. Students can use tree diagrams to find relationships among data and to review information to study for tests.

OVIPAROUS ANIMALS							
Vertebrates				Invertebrates			
legs		legless		legs		legless	
amphibians	birds	reptiles	fish	arthropods	insects	mollusks	echinoderm
toad salamander	woodpecker chickens ostrich	snake	bass shark seahorse	spider tarantula	grasshopper beetles moths	snail clam oyster	starfish sea urchin

Reflections
I used a tree chart to organize my science notes.
I was able to classify all the oviparous animals we studied except the Duckbill Platypus and the Spiny Anteater. I need to find out more about these two unusual Australian animals.

5

Share and Use Learning

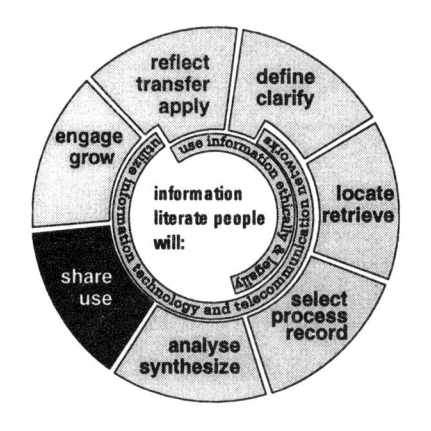

Students require many opportunities to share and apply what they have learned.

They choose an appropriate format for sharing by

☆ brainstorming a variety of ways to share
☆ evaluating the advantages and disadvantages of the various formats*
☆ deciding on the best format for sharing, considering
　☆ their personal talents and skills
　☆ the audience

Students prepare a draft by

☆ making a plan
☆ gathering all the materials and equipment needed
☆ addressing all the assignment criteria

They create the product or presentation by

☆ using the gathered information and their original ideas to create something new
☆ using such appropriate technologies as computers, tape recorders, cameras*

Students share or use the results by

☆ practising the presentation or application
☆ paying attention to good presentation/production skills
☆ using technologies where appropriate*

---

* Younger students will need assistance in doing this.

Answering Questions and Sharing Learning

Your students have collected their data and discovered some fascinating information. Now they are ready to answer their inquiry question and share their learning with others. They need to find the most effective format for sharing their discoveries.

In the early years, students require many opportunities to practise simplified versions of the same variety of presentations that older students use.

Suppose that your class has just completed a study of Wild Animals of North America. You would begin with one medium and create a collaborative class presentation.

Each child could be assigned one letter of the alphabet and asked to select an animal. They would each create an illustration and a few written facts about that animal: its food, habitat, habits, and so on. The final presentation would be a book that the students could share with learning buddies, peers, etc., each student taking a turn to read her or his own page and explain the significance of the illustration. The students would be involved in the planning process through charting its stages and their corresponding responsibilities.

This same strategy transfers well to use with computer software to create a slide show or HyperCard stack to save and share with others.

Creating Something New

The students should progress through a broad range of experiences, ultimately creating products and presentations that require additional synthesis and are thus more effective... and more fun.

Now you need to help students progress from a simple retelling of facts to applying those facts to create something new.

Teach them to weave the facts into a fictional story about the animal that includes the facts or attributes the factual characteristics. First, be sure that students understand the similarities and differences between fact and fiction (see page 44).

Then create a group chart using information students learned in their animal study. On the chart, list the facts that the students plan to use.

☆ a bear cub is playing in its den
☆ familiar with only dried leaves and grass
☆ finds the outside world
☆ discovers real live grass and leaves
☆ catches salmon for dinner
☆ dodges bees to get honey for dessert

Create the story. Model this process a number of times prior to letting students attempt it on their own.

Be sure to allow students lots of time to talk and share their learning.

Further Presentation Ideas

This storyline could become the script for a puppet play that students perform for others. You might videotape the show to share and critique later.

The facts about an animal and its predators could be used to create a board game based on Snakes and Ladders.

The story could be turned into a rebus.

Select some words related to the animal, brainstorm other words that rhyme with these and create rhyming verse … For additional presentation ideas, see Share Your Talents, page 72.

Considering Multiple Intelligences

Everyone learns in different ways. When students are deciding on a format for their products and presentations, you'll want to guide them in picking the one they're most comfortable with and that best demonstrates their talents. Conversely, being aware of students' multiple intelligences could also mean that you encourage them to choose a presentation format that allows them to develop in new areas. Page 68 will help students in considering their multiple intelligences.

My Multiple Intelligences

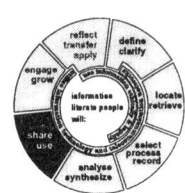

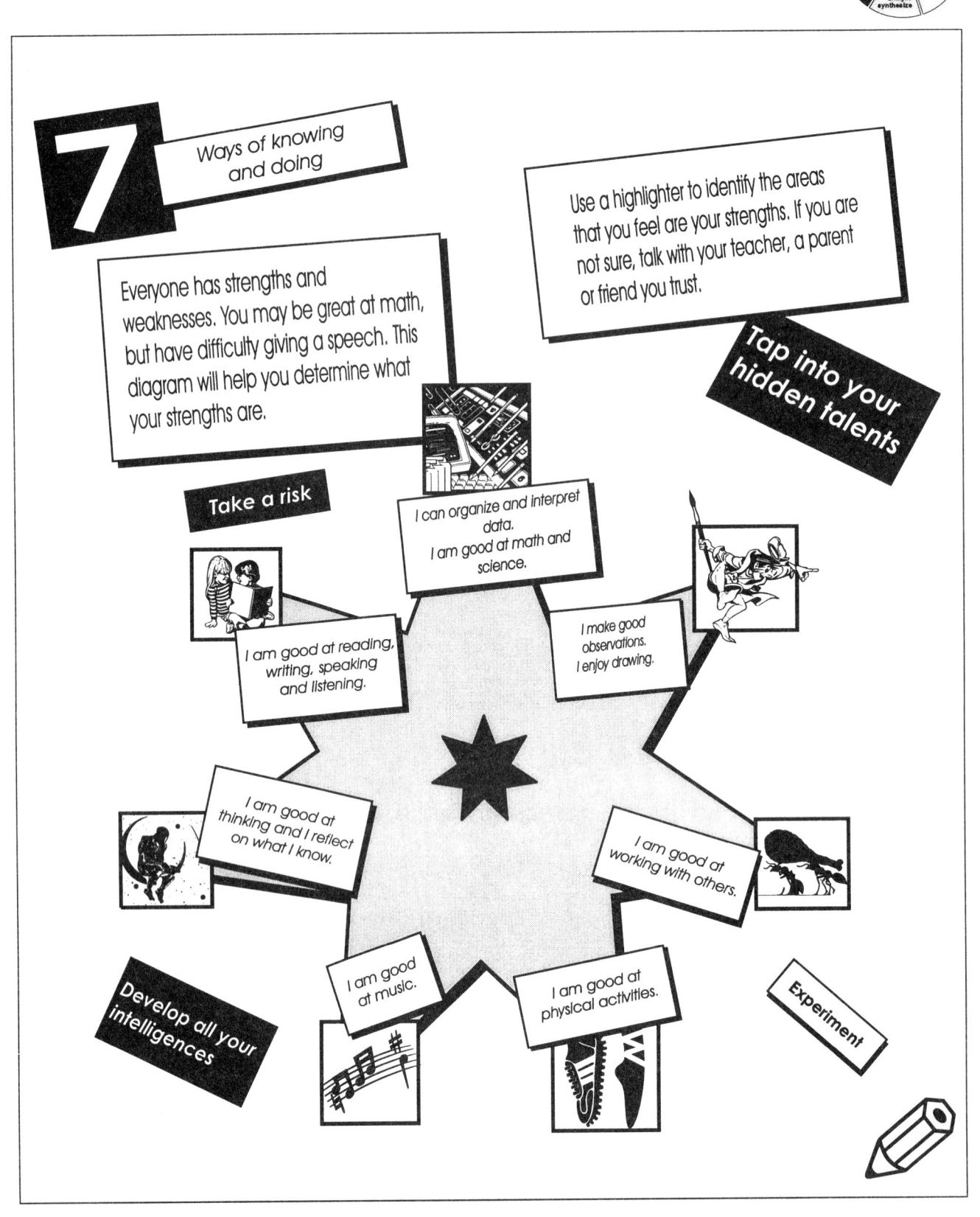

7 Ways of knowing and doing

Everyone has strengths and weaknesses. You may be great at math, but have difficulty giving a speech. This diagram will help you determine what your strengths are.

Use a highlighter to identify the areas that you feel are your strengths. If you are not sure, talk with your teacher, a parent or friend you trust.

Tap into your hidden talents

Take a risk

- I can organize and interpret data. I am good at math and science.
- I am good at reading, writing, speaking and listening.
- I make good observations. I enjoy drawing.
- I am good at thinking and I reflect on what I know.
- I am good at working with others.
- I am good at music.
- I am good at physical activities.

Develop all your intelligences

Experiment

68

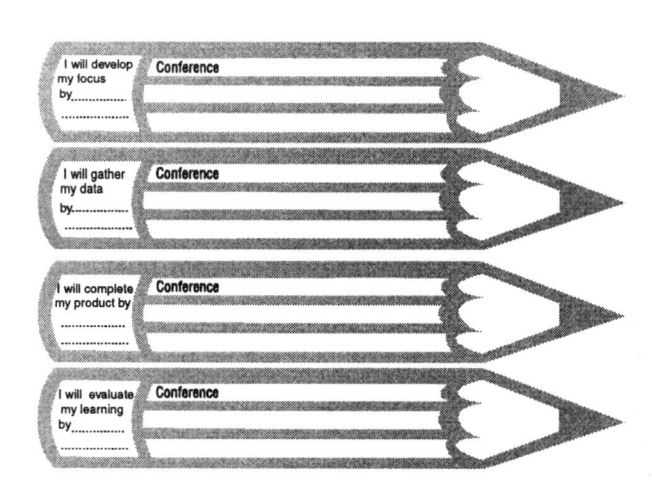

Developing Skills Self-Awareness

As students become more independent and begin to create individual presentations, they will develop a growing awareness of their own skills, talents and interests. This will help them make informed decisions when creating products and presentations. Completing Learning About Yourself surveys like the one on page 85 will help in this process of self-awareness.

Planning Presentations

As students begin to create their own presentations, they must learn to plan the content, materials and time lines. An organizer such as this Action Plan for Presentations will help guide their planning. Setting times and stages for teacher and student conferences is crucial to student success. A contract for conferencing will help keep the students on track.

The following reproducible pages will help students plan their products and presentations.

Topic Wetlands   **Teachers** Mrs Mallin and Ms. Braithwaite

Focus (question or purpose)
How does the body of the mudskipper compare to that of the frog?

Format for sharing Puppet show

Date of presentation May 10   **Location** Library Information Centre

Criteria to be met (time, content, evaluation, etc.)	How will I meet these criteria?
Content – Include all the information necessary to answer the question completely – logical order – accurate facts	– write the script so that it has all the information about my subtopics – check the script with dot-jots on my organizer
Length – 5 minutes	– time it when I practise, and shorten or lengthen it
Evaluation – copy of script – keep audience attention – information easy to understand – clear visuals, large enough – loud enough – 2 or more media	– make an extra copy of the play – add a little humour – test out on some friends or family – use audio of wetland sounds – puppets and script – wetlands visuals
Materials needed – puppets, puppet stage – audiotape of wetland sounds	– collect materials and make puppets of a frog and a mudskipper – plan time for practices; plan when to finish – make arrangements with the teacher-librarian
Experts who can help me – drama club puppeteers – librarian	– ask for puppeteer helpers

Pencil-shaped conference tracking:
- I will develop my focus by........   Conference
- I will gather my data by........   Conference
- I will complete my product by........   Conference
- I will evaluate my learning by........   Conference

My Sharing Plan

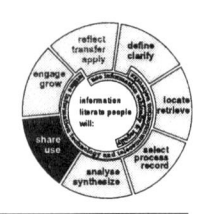

❏ I have found lots of information about _____.

❏ I have thought about my discoveries.

❏ I am ready to share my learning.

I am good at

❏ drawing / painting ❏ writing

❏ building things ❏ singing

❏ pretending ❏ telling stories

❏ computer work ❏ acting

I will share my learning by _____
_____
_____

I will need to get _____
_____
_____

I will need help with _____
_____
_____

Name . . . .

So What...?

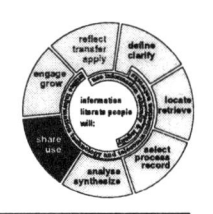

**Now I've collected all this information and I've figured out my personal strengths ...
How will I use it?**

Be adventurous

Write a play, poem, diary ...
Create a video, Web page, dance ...
Invent a game, puzzle, tool ...
Compose a rap, routine, rebus ...
Develop a theory, formula, HyperCard stack ...
Design a costume, pamphlet, blueprint ...
Construct a model, project cube, prototype ...
Plan a newscast, simulation, slideshow ...

Predict a solution, trend, pattern ...

Try something different

71

Share Your Talents

Share Your Talents

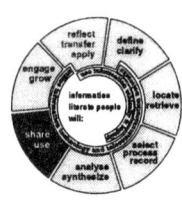

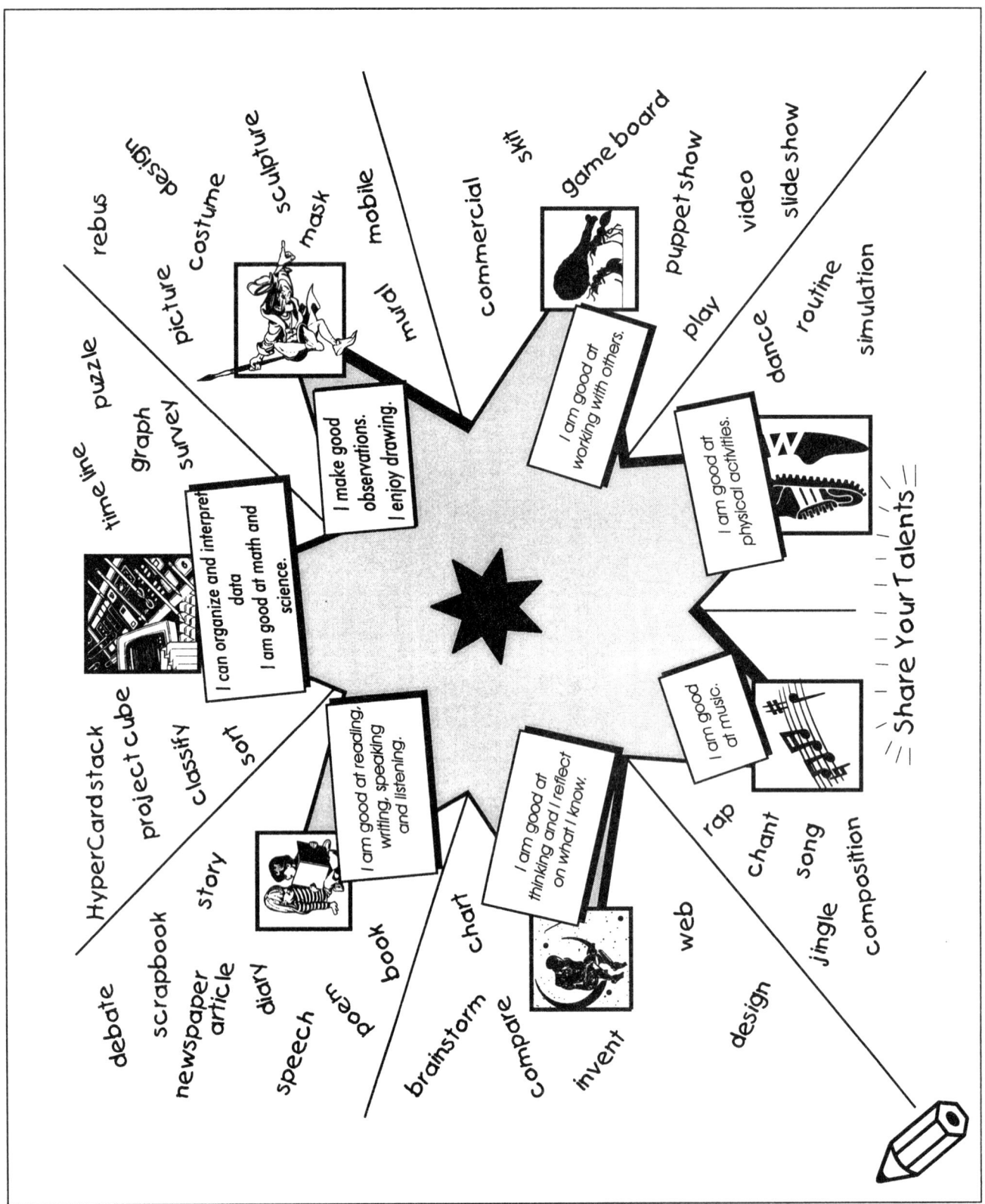

I am good at working with others.
commercial, skit, game board, puppet show, play, video, slide show, dance, routine, simulation

I am good at physical activities.

I am good at music.
rap, chant, song, jingle, composition

I am good at thinking and I reflect on what I know.
brainstorm, compare, invent, web, design, chart

I am good at reading, writing, speaking and listening.
debate, scrapbook, newspaper article, diary, speech, poem, story, book

I can organize and interpret data. I am good at math and science.
HyperCard stack, project cube, classify, sort, time line, puzzle, graph, survey

I make good observations. I enjoy drawing.
rebus, design, picture, costume, sculpture, mask, mural, mobile

72

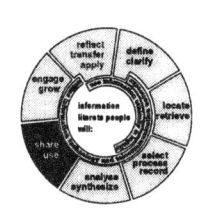

Presentation Cube

Clip the shape.
Fold on the dotted lines.
Create a cube.

Prepare for questions about your presentation.

Consider your audience!

✔ Check off each stage as you complete it.

PRESENTATION TIPS
- ❏ make a plan
- ❏ organize information
- ❏ create a dynamic introduction
- ❏ a strong concluding statement summarizes the main points
- ❏ edit all written work

WRITTEN
- ❏ organize subtopics in paragraphs
- ❏ create a powerful introduction and conclusion
- ❏ write your final draft on a computer
- ❏ keep a copy
- ❏ think about how to present information visually

VISUAL
- ❏ build your project to last
- ❏ organize information
- ❏ create a dynamic introduction
- ❏ a strong concluding statement summarizes the main points
- ❏ edit all written work

ORAL
- ❏ prepare cue cards
- ❏ rehearse (mirror, video camera, tape recorder)
- ❏ practise using a microphone if necessary
- ❏ time your presentation
- ❏ gather and test AV equipment

MULTIMEDIA
- ❏ make a plan (media board)
- ❏ consult experts
- ❏ use technologies effectively
- ❏ test, practise, rehearse
- ❏ time your presentation
- ❏ check equipment

I could use a larger version of this cube to display my visuals and the cues for my presentation.

Writing for Various Purposes and Audiences

Students need many occasions to write for a variety of purposes and audiences. A written component of a research project is an authentic application of the writing process. It offers an authentic opportunity to take written work to the published stage.

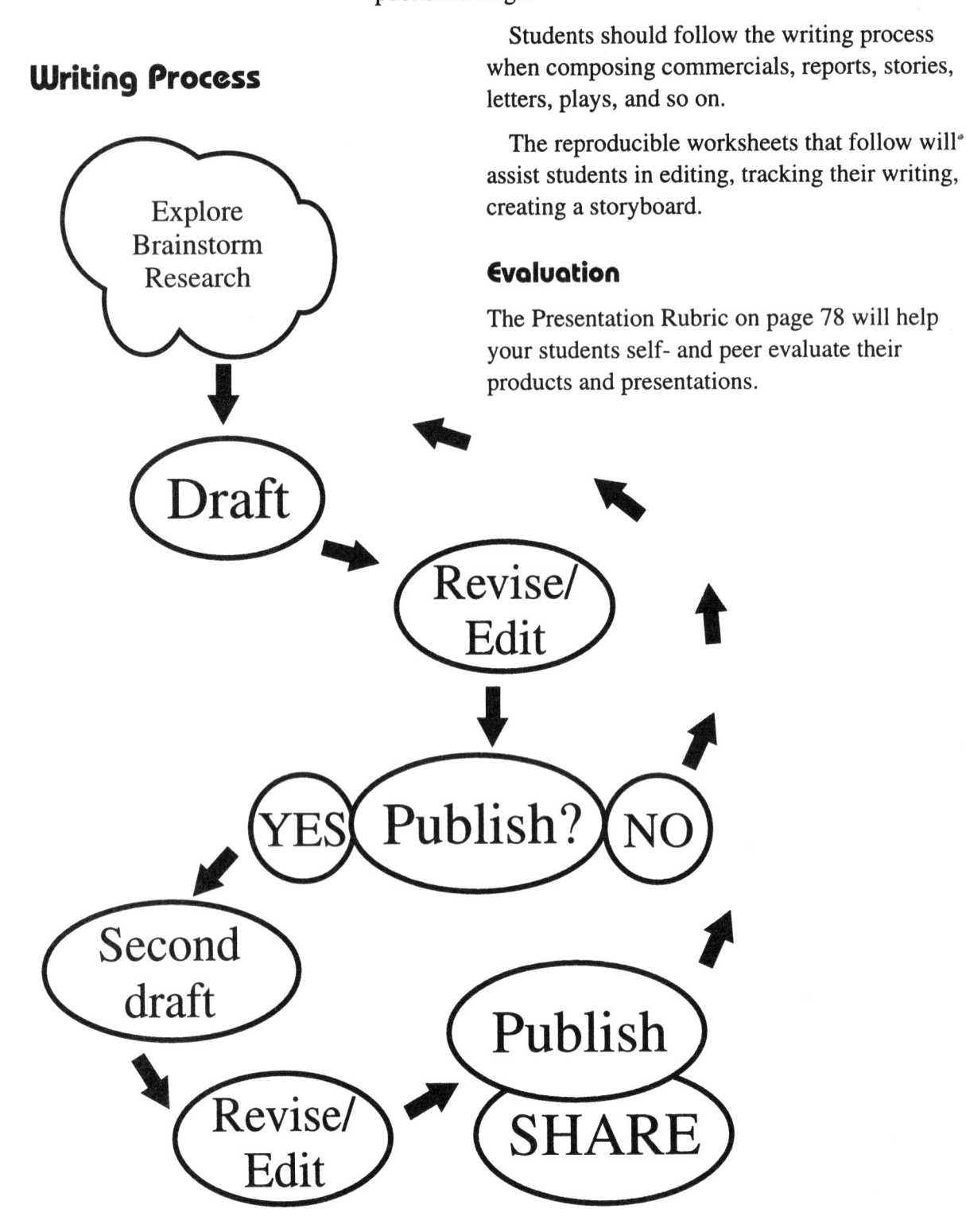

Students should follow the writing process when composing commercials, reports, stories, letters, plays, and so on.

The reproducible worksheets that follow will assist students in editing, tracking their writing, creating a storyboard.

Evaluation

The Presentation Rubric on page 78 will help your students self- and peer evaluate their products and presentations.

Writing Process

- Explore Brainstorm Research
- Draft
- Revise/Edit
- Publish? YES / NO
- Second draft
- Revise/Edit
- Publish SHARE

Editing Tips

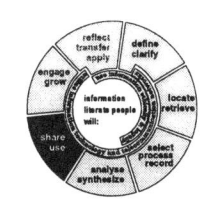

The editing pencil is in the hand of the Author!

Read your work 3 times!

1. for meaning ✔
2. for punctuation ✔
3. for spelling ✔

Spell ✔ Warning

✔ Spell check will not find words that are spelled correctly but used incorrectly.
[*Such as: "Tom **through** the juggling ball." or "I am **form** Alberta."*]

✔ Not sure, use a dictionary!

✔ Print a hard copy to edit. Make changes using **cut**, **paste** and **copy** features.

Editing Symbols

^	Insert word
?	Meaning
(thay)	Spelling
canada	Capital
~~nice~~	Delete
⌒,⌒	Punctuation needed

75

Tracking My Writing

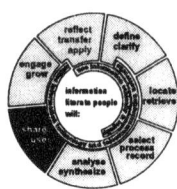

Prewriting
- ❏ focus
- ❏ brainstorm
- ❏ research

Draft
I will
- ❏ conference about my idea
- ❏ make a plan
- ❏ write on paper or word processor
- ❏ use every other line or double space
- ❏ write, write, write

How can I improve my draft?

Revise
I can
- ❏ make a strong beginning sentence
- ❏ check for overused words
- ❏ take some ideas out
- ❏ change some ideas
- ❏ add some ideas
- ❏ rearrange some ideas
- ❏ make sure my writing makes sense
- ❏ make a strong ending sentence

Edit
- ❏ check punctuation
- ❏ check spelling
- ❏ make sure each sentence makes sense
- ❏ use editing symbols
- ❏ conference with a learning partner or teacher

Using a word processing program on a computer makes revising and editing **faster, neater,** and **easier**.

Storyboard It!

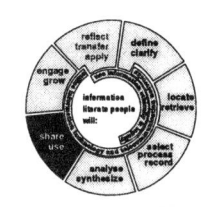

You can use a **storyboard** to help you create a cartoon, storybook, radio or TV commercial, puppet play, video, filmstrip … Just draw a picture in the **frame** for each episode in your story. Then write the **script** to tell what's happening in each frame. Be sure to number your frames.

Frame   **Script**

77

Presentation Rubric

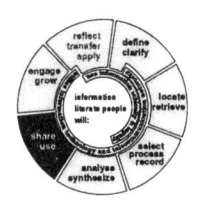

Peer Evaluation

Get ready for questions. One way you will know that you've made a good presentation is that your audience is as interested in your topic as you are. Here is a sample form for evaluating a presentation.

Category	Low	Middle	High
Information	limited information	good information, but needed more sources	rich information shows original thinking
Organization	information disorganized	some organization of information	information presented in a logical manner
Understanding	limited understanding	able to answer some questions	able to fully answer questions and add additional information
Originality	predictable	some original aspects	highly original presentation
Audience	did not keep the audience's attention	audience was interested some of the time	the audience was fully engaged and learned new ideas/information
Group Work	unable to work cooperatively	members of the group participated	members of the group worked as a productive and supportive team

Name .... Date ....

78

6

Engage in Literary and Media Experiences

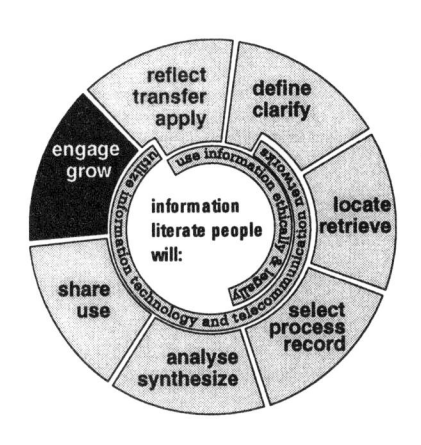

As well as listening, reading and viewing for information, students need to experience literature and media for personal growth and enjoyment.

Students select literature (stories, chapter books, picture books, novels, poems) and media texts (television programs, videos, magazines, plays, CD-ROMs, newspapers)

☆ based on personal likes and dislikes
☆ to meet their entertainment and information needs
☆ in a variety of types and genres

They read, view and listen to an assortment of materials for information and pleasure. In so doing, students

☆ express and defend their personal opinions
☆ respect the preferences of others
☆ keep a log of their literature and media experiences
☆ react to characters, events, authors
☆ make connections between story and personal experiences

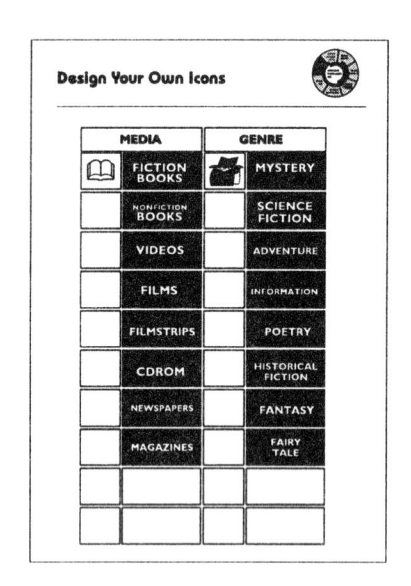

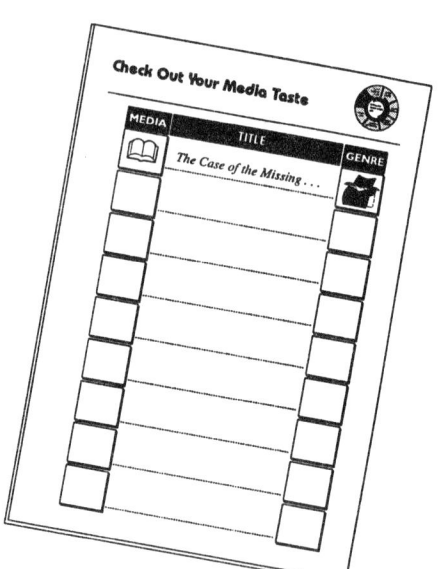

Personal Selection Criteria

Over time, students will develop their own personal taste in genre. They will learn to identify what they like about certain pieces and be able to explain their preferences.

To help students discover the genres that give them the greatest enjoyment, encourage them to keep a log of personal reading, viewing and listening habits. The sheet on page 81 can be used to facilitate student logging.

Having students complete a Taste Test will help them track what they read and view and record their reactions to various genres.

Helping Students Make Personal Connections

Children innately search for themselves in stories they read, view or listen to. You can use this healthy celebration of self as a starting point for writing, talking and thinking.

The organizers on pages 82 through 85 will assist students in expressing personal responses and making connections with story characters.

Critical Thinking

Even young students can begin to function as critics in evaluating the success of an author's craft.

Taste Test

Media \ Genre	Novels	Short Stories	Movies	T.V.	
Mystery		I	II	||||	8
Time Travel	I		II	I	4
Realism	II	I	I	II	6
Comedy	II	I		|||| II	10
	5	3	5	15	

I enjoy mysteries on television.
I should try reading some.

Reading Log

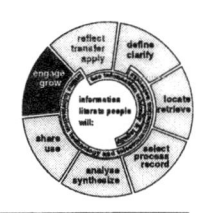

Date	Best Part ....
	....
Title	....
	Quotes ....
Author	....
Genre	

Date	Best Part ....
	....
Title	....
	Quotes ....
Author	....
Genre	

Date	Best Part ....
	....
Title	....
	Quotes ....
Author	....
Genre	

Date	Best Part ....
	....
Title	....
	Quotes ....
Author	....
Genre	

Name ....

Personal Response to Story

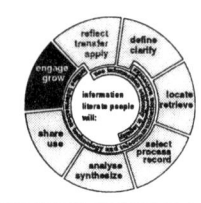

Use a combination of one phrase from each column to help you give your personal responses to the story.

For example:

I laughed when _____

_____

_____ . It reminded me of

_____ .

Feeling

I laughed when
I cried when
I held my breath when
I smiled when
I was scared when
I was happy when
I was worried when
I was excited when

Association

I thought
I hoped
If that happened to me
I could imagine I
It was like when I
It felt like when
It reminded me of
I would never

Setting and Time

The setting is where the story happened. It could be in the local mall, in the desert, on a movie set, at the hospital, in outer space...

The story could happen at a variety of different times as well. It could occur during one season, over a long period of time, in the distant past, recent past, or even in the future.

The setting of this story is _____

_____

This setting made it interesting for me because

_____

_____

_____

The time the story is set in is_____

This time makes it interesting because _____

_____

Use these ideas to create your own response organizer.

Making Personal Connections

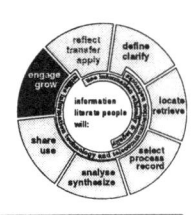

Reflecting on the characters

Title _____

I would like to be _____ because _____
_____
_____
_____

I'm glad I am not because _____
_____
_____
_____

I would like _____ for a friend (sister, brother, mom, dad...) because _____
_____
_____
_____

I wouldn't like _____ for a friend (sister, brother, mom, dad...) because _____
_____
_____
_____

If I could give _____ some advice I would suggest that
_____
_____
_____

Name . . . .

83

Character/Personal Journal

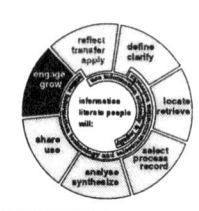

Date ....

Date ....

Date ....

Name ....

Learning About Yourself

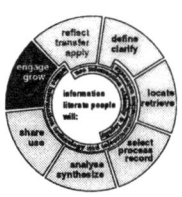

THINGS THAT SCARE ME

I like to learn about . . .

I want to be . . .

My Favourite Books

Reflecting on Feelings Using Time Lines

Time lines can be from the viewpoint of the reader or of any of the characters in the story.

This example is from *Brenda and Edward* by Maryann Kovalski.

Brenda

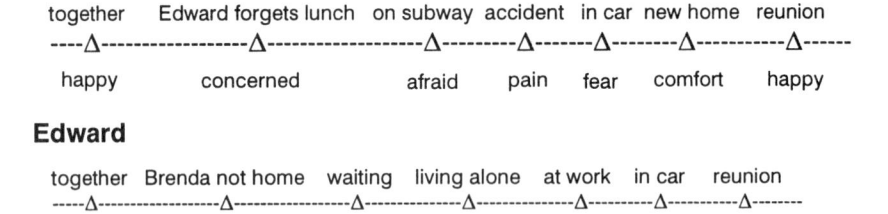

together	Edward forgets lunch	on subway	accident	in car	new home	reunion
happy	concerned	afraid	pain	fear	comfort	happy

Edward

together	Brenda not home	waiting	living alone	at work	in car	reunion
happy	worried annoyed	lonely angry	sad lonely	content proud	curious excited	happy

Assist students in comparing time lines from two different characters. After creating the time lines, using a graphic organizer such as a Venn diagram will help students see relationships and causes.

Connecting Reading, Viewing and Writing

The following skills are transferable to reading, viewing and also writing a story.

Prediction

Prediction enables students to get intimately involved in a story. They search for clues and hints and think about what these could mean. As they consider the characters involved and their possible motives, students can predict story events and a solution to a character's problem. (See pages 88 and 89.)

Problems and Solutions

When students get involved in a storyline and identify with a character, they discover that character's main problem. They examine cause and effect as they suggest solutions, choose the one they think best and confirm their predictions. (See page 90.)

Story Mapping

Story Mapping helps students get an overview of story elements and events. They can map a story's

☆ main characters and their personalities
☆ setting
☆ beginning, middle, ending
☆ problems and solutions

(See page 91.)

If your students think about what they read and view using organizers like these, they will discover how good stories are crafted. And when they use this same kind of organizer in planning their own writing, they will compose better stories.

Story Map

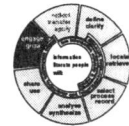

| Title | Author |

| Characters | Description | | Settings | Description |

Illustration

| Beginning | Middle | End |

Name

87

Solving the Mystery

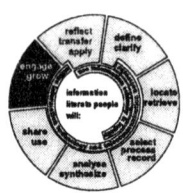

Title
Author
Detective

Motive ....
Suspects ....
Clue ....

Motive ....
Suspects ....
Clue ....

Motive ....
Suspects ....
Clue ....

My Solution ....

Name ....

Prediction Tree

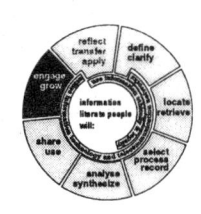

Prediction Tree

Prediction _ _ _ _ _ _
_ _ _ _ _ _ _ _ _ _
_ _ _ _ _ _ _ _ _ _
_ _ _ _ _ _ _ _ _ _

Hint _ _ _ _ _ _ _ _
_ _ _ _ _ _ _ _ _ _

Prediction _ _ _ _ _ _
_ _ _ _ _ _ _ _ _ _
_ _ _ _ _ _ _ _ _ _
_ _ _ _ _ _ _ _ _ _

Hint _ _ _ _ _ _ _ _
_ _ _ _ _ _ _ _ _ _

Event
_ _ _ _ _ _ _ _ _ _ _ _ _ _ _
_ _ _ _ _ _ _ _ _ _ _ _ _ _ _
_ _ _ _ _ _ _ _ _ _ _ _ _ _ _
_ _ _ _ _ _ _ _ _ _ _ _ _ _ _
_ _ _ _ _ _ _ _ _ _ _ _ _ _ _

Prediction _ _ _ _ _ _
_ _ _ _ _ _ _ _ _ _
_ _ _ _ _ _ _ _ _ _
_ _ _ _ _ _ _ _ _ _

Hint _ _ _ _ _ _ _ _
_ _ _ _ _ _ _ _ _ _

Prediction _ _ _ _ _ _
_ _ _ _ _ _ _ _ _ _
_ _ _ _ _ _ _ _ _ _
_ _ _ _ _ _ _ _ _ _

Hint _ _ _ _ _ _ _ _
_ _ _ _ _ _ _ _ _ _

Prediction _ _ _ _ _ _
_ _ _ _ _ _ _ _ _ _
_ _ _ _ _ _ _ _ _ _
_ _ _ _ _ _ _ _ _ _

Hint _ _ _ _ _ _ _ _
_ _ _ _ _ _ _ _ _ _

Prediction _ _ _ _ _ _
_ _ _ _ _ _ _ _ _ _
_ _ _ _ _ _ _ _ _ _
_ _ _ _ _ _ _ _ _ _

Hint _ _ _ _ _ _ _ _
_ _ _ _ _ _ _ _ _ _

Name . . . . Date . . . .

This Is the Problem

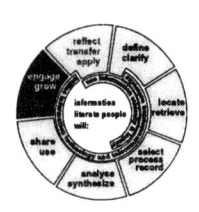

Problem _____

Cause _____   Effect _____
_____   _____
_____   _____

Solution #1 | But it didn't work!

Solution #2 | But it didn't work!

Solution #3 | But it didn't work!

Solution #4 | Finally it worked because . . .

What Was The Character Feeling And Thinking?

Name ....

Story Map Planner

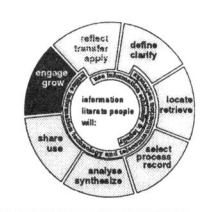

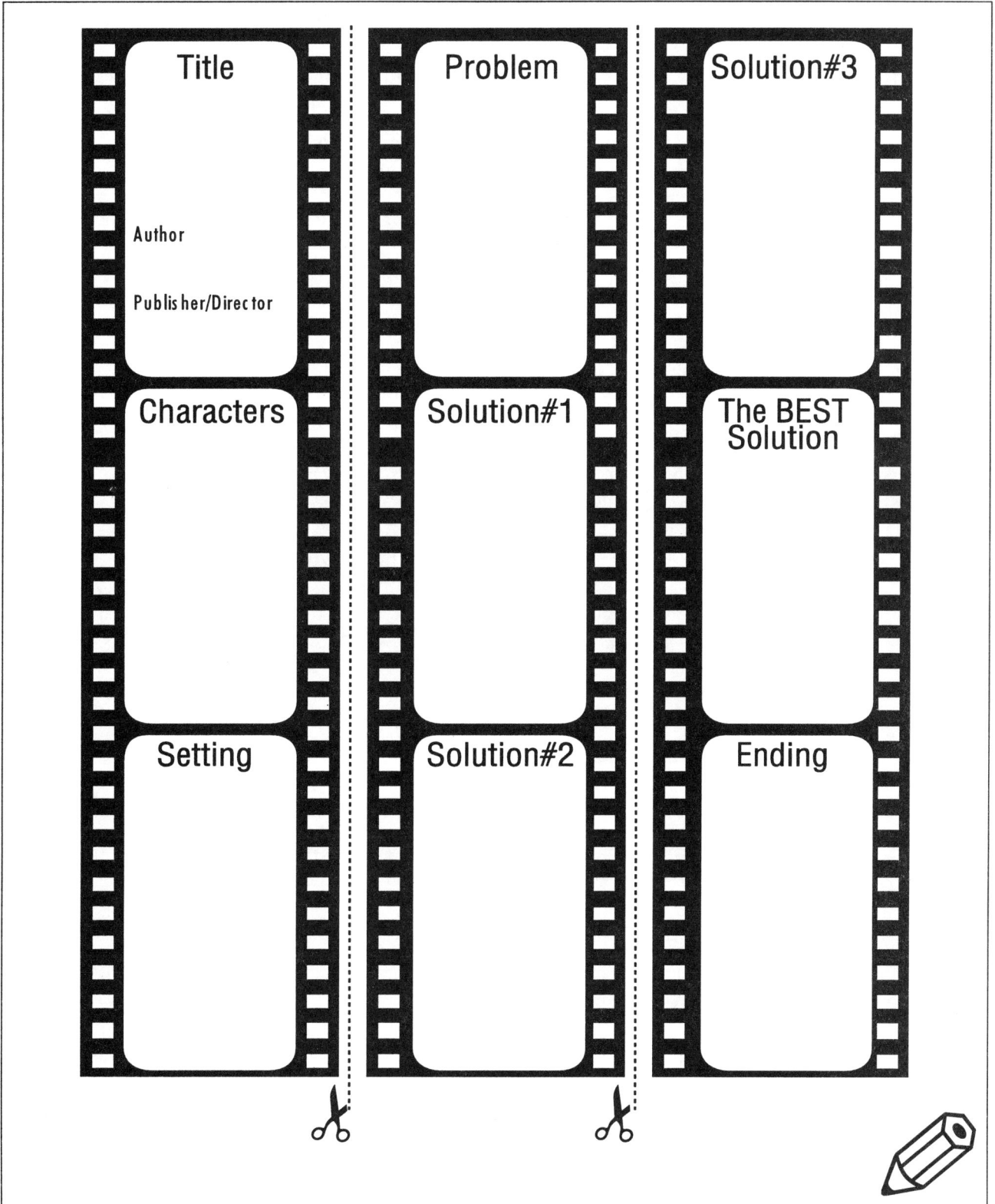

Title	Problem	Solution #3
Author		
Publisher/Director		
Characters	Solution #1	The BEST Solution
Setting	Solution #2	Ending

Comparing Versions

Students can gain a deeper understanding of story structure and technique by comparing different versions of the same story. They can compare and contrast

- ☆ versions of the same story by two different authors
- ☆ a book and its video adaptation
- ☆ a book and its story's retelling by a storyteller
- ☆ a book and its stage adaptation (play)

Students can explore the following questions.

- ☆ What stayed the same?
- ☆ What changed? How is it different?
- ☆ Why was it changed? Was the producer/author trying to make it
  - ☆ more interesting, exciting?
  - ☆ appeal to a different audience?

They can use an organizer like the one on page 93 or a Venn diagram to compare and contrast versions.

Analysis

Encourage your students to express their own opinions in answering

- ☆ Were the changes successful?
- ☆ Did they improve the story? Why or why not?
- ☆ Did they harm it? If so, how and why?
- ☆ What changes were enabled by the medium being used?

Students might consider this famous quotation:

"Don't wait for the movie. Read the book."

What do they think of this statement? Why?

Deconstructing Media

Invite students to consider the strategies a media producer uses to influence the audience. Ask them about their viewing experience.

- ☆ How did you feel? Why?
- ☆ How did you react? Why?
- ☆ What do you believe? Why?
- ☆ What do you think is important? Why?
- ☆ Did the audio affect you? How? Why?

Students can use an organizer like the one on page 94 in deconstructing a media production.

Subject: advertisement for jeans   Name: Julia

	Camera Techniques	Evidence	Effect
Criteria	close up shots	faces of teenagers smiling and laughing, labels on jeans	viewer feels part of action
Criteria	blurred and distant	those not included not wearing "the" jeans	very impressive • important
	Sound Track	**Evidence**	**Effect**
Criteria	music selected to appeal to target group	sounds like current popular song	teenagers relate to it
Criteria	used to catch attention	music is louder than speaking	we are likely to agree
	Appeal to Emotions	**Evidence**	**Effect**
Criteria	personal popularity	the girl all the boys follow is wearing "the" jeans	to be popular I must wear these jeans
Criteria	need to feel wanted	girl left behind & ignored wears another brand	if I don't have these jeans I'll be left out

So What? this company is trying to make me believe I will be a social outcast if I don't wear their jeans.

I know that's not true. Many personal characteristics determine my popularity.

Compare and Contrast

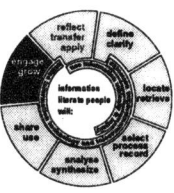

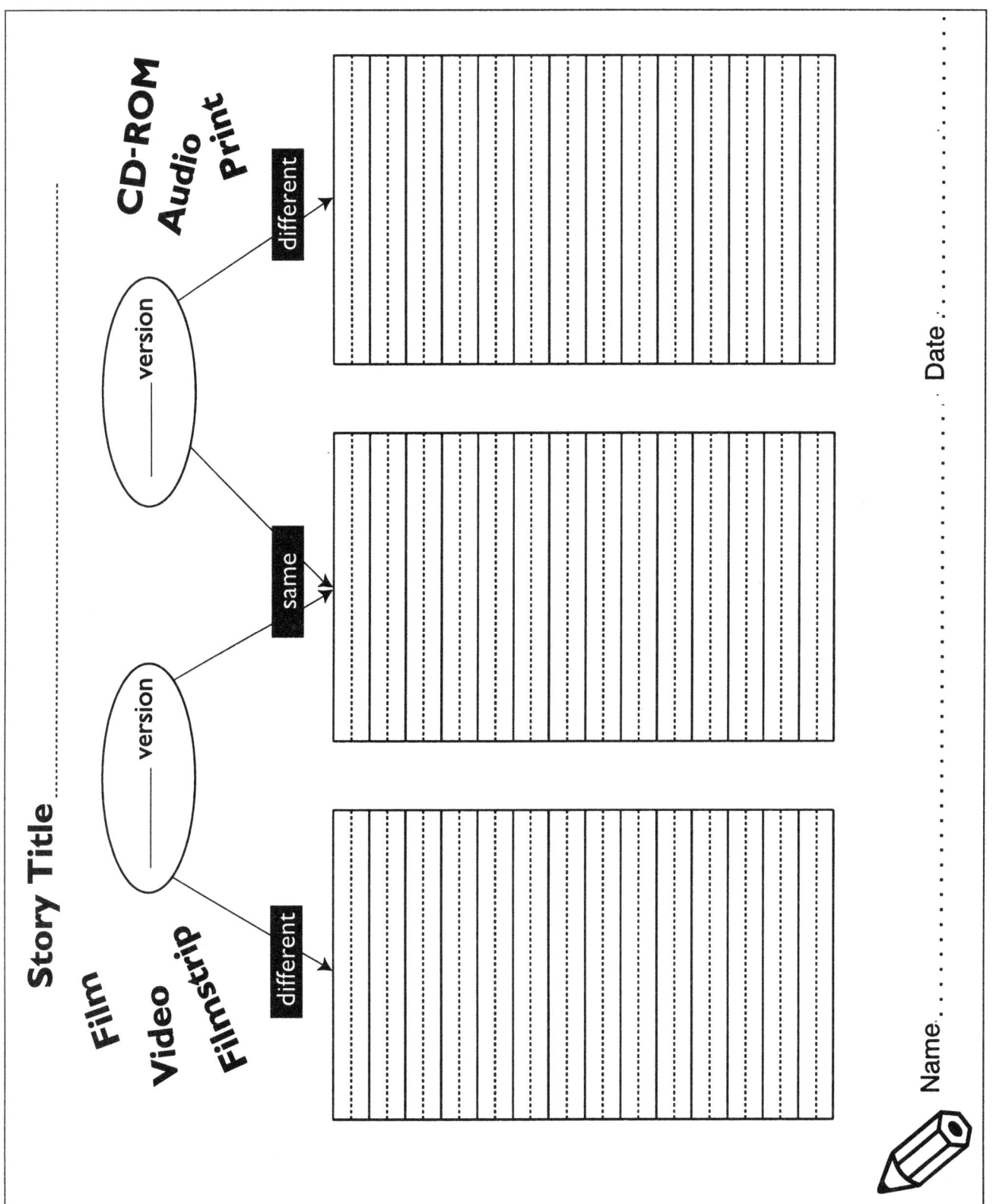

Story Title _____

CD-ROM
Audio
Print

___ version

different →

same →

Film
Video
Filmstrip

___ version

different →

Name. _____ Date _____

93

Deconstructing Media

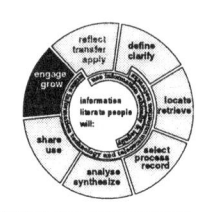

	Camera Techniques	Evidence	Effect
Criteria ❶ ❷			

	Sound Track	Evidence	Effect
Criteria ❶ ❷			

	Appeal to Emotions	Evidence	Effect
Criteria ❶ ❷			

So What?

Name ....

Using Literature to Develop Thinking Skills

Problem Solving

Many picture books are structured around a problem, several attempted solutions and the one that finally solves the problem to everyone's satisfaction. Children's authors often use this pattern as a framework for their storylines. *Franklin in the Dark* by Paulette Bourgeois is an example of a story which follows the problem solving model.

Storybooks are best read for the sheer enjoyment of the story itself. Because story is so engaging however, we should take advantage of its powerful appeal to, once in a while, lead children into story extensions that exercise their thinking skills.

You can use the following procedure to model story analysis.

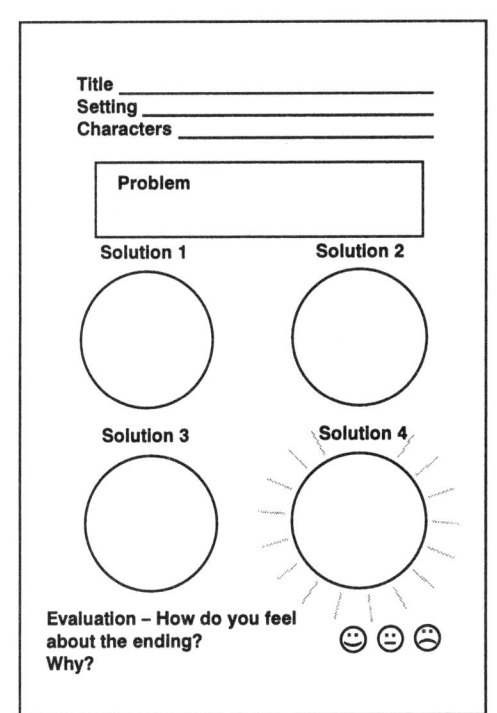

Read: *Franklin in the Dark.*

Interact:

☆ Read the pictures.
☆ Talk about feelings.
☆ Enjoy, Enjoy!

Franklin has a big problem. What is it?

Create a chart.

What did he try first to overcome his fear?
Second?
Third?
What was the best solution?

How do you feel about the ending?

Model this analysis exercise for lots of books that have a problem solving storyline.

Once your students are familiar with the process, they can use a problem solving organizer like the one on this page as a planner for composing their own stories.

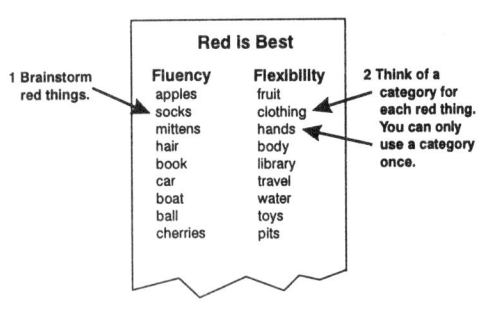

Fluency and Flexibility

Fluency and flexibility are crucial attributes of lifelong learners. Even very young students can benefit from practising fluency and flexibility. Here is a sample exercise:

What is your favourite colour? If it is red, you will love *Red Is Best* by Kathy Stinson. The language in this story is particularly beautiful and engaging for young children. Enjoy first; then build on the language.

Tip: Experience with fluency and flexibility exercises is a prerequisite for webbing.

```
                  Red Is Best
1 Brainstorm   Fluency    Flexibility   2 Think of a
  red things.  apples     fruit           category for
               socks      clothing        each red thing.
               mittens    hands           You can only
               hair       body            use a category
               book       library         once.
               car        travel
               boat       water
               ball       toys
               cherries   pits
```

Decision Making

Exercises in evaluating possible story solutions and deciding on the best one assist children in developing their decision making skills. For example:

Read: *Dog's Breath* by Dave Pilkey and meet Hallytosis, a dog with a real problem. If you don't read the pictures, you will miss a lot!

Brainstorm (in small groups):

☆ ways to cure Hally's breath

Evaluate (whole group):

☆ decide on criteria for evaluating solutions
☆ decide on a scale
☆ each group uses a cross-reference chart to record solutions and criteria
☆ score
☆ decide

Solutions / Criteria	chop up breath mints in the dog food	teach the dog to floss	replace teeth with dentures
cost	5	5	0
safety	5	3	0
reality	4	0	0

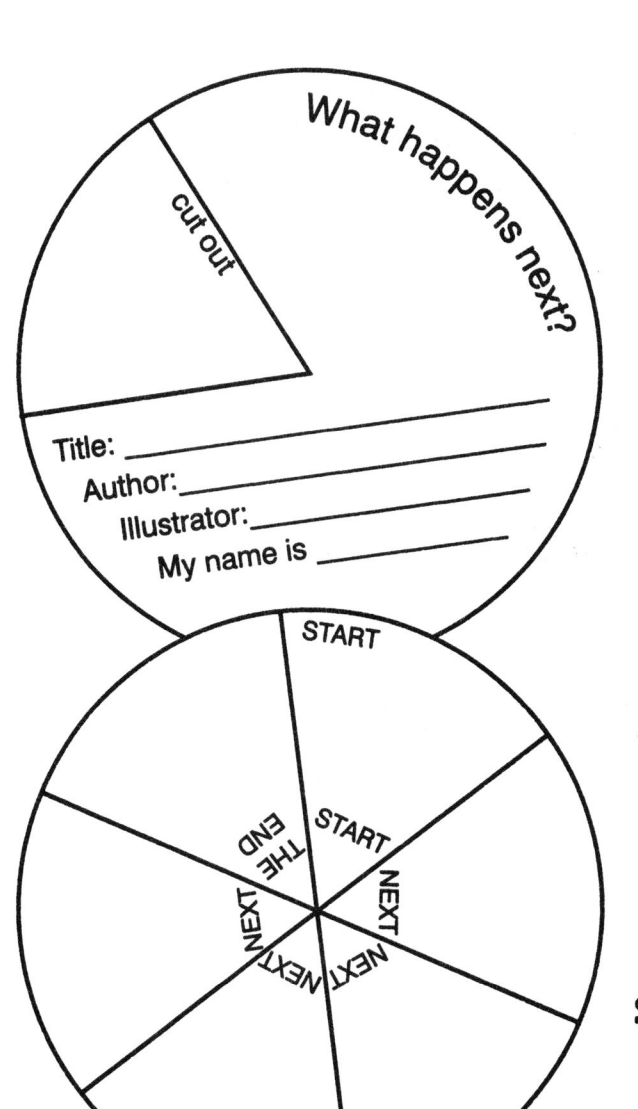

Sequencing and Story Mapping

Prereaders and special-needs students can use drawings to map the sequence of events in a story. Here are some graphic organizers for mapping and sequencing.

Clothesline Story

Use the Clothesline Story strategy for telling, retelling, visual clues to create new stories, and so on. Your students will want to develop their own clothesline stories

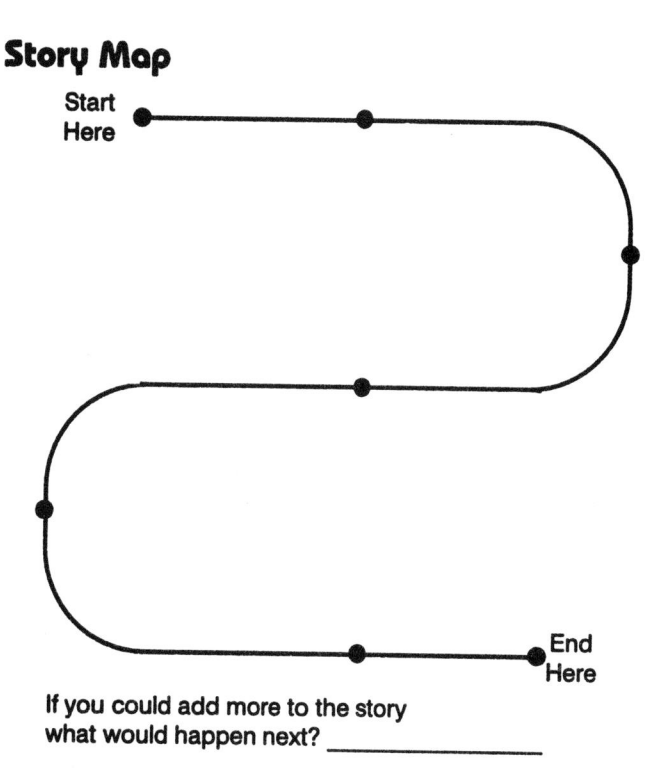

What happens next?

cut out

Title: _____
Author: _____
Illustrator: _____
My name is _____

START
NEXT
NEXT
THE END
START
NEXT
NEXT

Story Map

Start Here

End Here

If you could add more to the story what would happen next? _____

Using Video to Develop Thinking, Visual and Language Skills

"Children and adults feel their interest quicken when moving pictures and sound can present language more comprehensively than any other teaching medium, and more realistically too. Using a video sequence in class is the next-best thing to experiencing the sequence in real life. In addition, video can take your students into the lives and experiences of others."

— *Stempleski and Tomlin, 1990*

Video in the Curriculum

Video provides a host of benefits for your curriculum. Using video will

☆ motivate students' interest in learning
☆ extend the range of classroom experiences
☆ supply relevant background information
☆ confirm students' prior knowledge and review information
☆ address a variety of learning styles and multiple intelligences
☆ level the "playing field" — all students will have the same background experience

The worksheet on the next page was designed for use with *Owl Moon*, a 9-minute video based on a picture book by Jane Yolen. The video is narrated by the author, with music by Ernest Troost. In *Owl Moon*, a father and his young daughter trek through a snowy landscape in search of the great horned owl. This heartwarming story is told from the perspective of the young girl. The video is suitable for both a Primary and Junior audience.

The questions could be modified for use with a variety of videos.

View a Video: Owl Moon

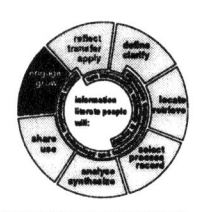

Watch the short video *Owl Moon* and enjoy the story, images and music.

Second Viewing

View *Owl Moon* again to find 4 things that you need to remember when you go owling.

If you go owling, you _____
- ☆ have to be brave
- ☆ make your own heat
- ☆ must be quiet

After Second Viewing

1 List 3 things you would add to the list of things you would need to remember if you went owling.

   1. _____
   2. _____
   3. _____

2 Why did they have to go owling "long after the child's bedtime"?

   _____
   _____
   _____

Third Viewing

3 Watch the video again to find examples of imagery.

   _____
   _____
   _____

4 Complete these phrases.

   1. as quiet as a _____
   2. still as _____
   3. cold, as if someone's icy hand was _____
   4. whiter than _____

99

7

Reflect on, Transfer and Apply Learning

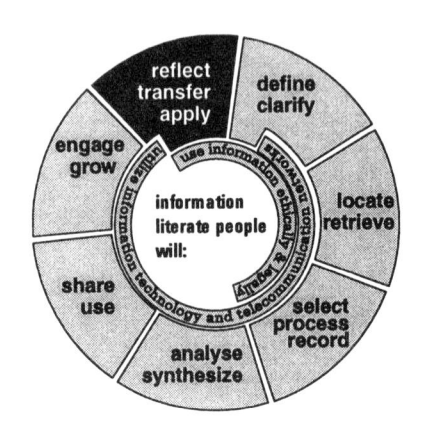

Students need to reflect on the research process, its products and their own learning. They should be given opportunities to transfer and apply their learning to new situations.

Students reflect on both process (the "how") and product (the "what") by

☆ using a learning log
☆ participating in self- and peer evaluation, using established criteria

They reflect on self-improvement by

☆ assessing their personal effort based on established criteria
☆ identifying areas for improvement
☆ setting goals for self-improvement
☆ planning action for self-improvement
☆ developing time-management skills*
☆ assessing and improving their study habits*

Students make personal connections by

☆ viewing issues from a variety of perspectives
☆ asking what the learning means to them*
　　☆ their family*
　　☆ their community*
　　☆ the world*

They apply their learning by

☆ suggesting what action should be taken
☆ initiating a response or action
☆ using new learning in another situation
☆ using new skills in a different situation

---

* These strategies will be more appropriate for Junior and Intermediate level students.

Making Skills Connections

Learning to learn is a process of developing skills and gaining independence in their application. When students make connections between skills they have learned in school and how those skills transfer to real-life situations, they are well on their way to becoming lifelong learners. As teachers, we can facilitate this development by challenging our students to make that transfer. When we model this process through integrated studies, our students experience authentic connections that are relevant and realistic.

Teaching Tools integrates information literacy, information technology and thinking skills. Thus you will have noticed that on occasion the same, or similar, graphic organizer appears in more than one stage. For instance, Venn diagrams are used in both Select, Process and Record Relevant Data (stage 3) and Analyse and Synthesize Information (stage 4). There is some overlap in the information accessing process; when students record their information on this type of organizer, they are in fact beginning to analyse it.

Transferring Skills and Thinking Critically

Analysing Resources

Using an organizer such as Finding the Best Materials for Me will help students determine the usefulness of a resource. It can guide them through the process of analysing a resource and making a decision about its appropriateness. Students are transferring their skills in analysis and decision making.

Critical Thinking in Lifelong Learning

Your students are using analysis and decision making skills in the selection and recording of information. As students master this kind of skill transfer, they are becoming lifelong learners who can adapt quickly to change and learn independently. Employers today tell us that they need people who are self-directed, who can

☆ think critically
☆ define and solve problems
☆ work cooperatively and collaboratively
☆ process and manage information
☆ apply knowledge to new situations
☆ take initiative
☆ use technologies effectively

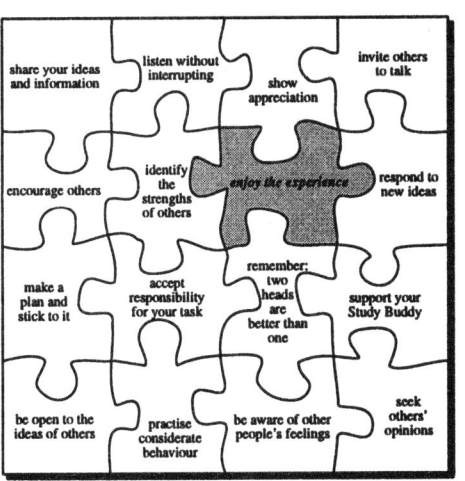

Modelling Problem Solving Skill Transference

You can model the use of the research process in problem solving applications other than a research project.

Invite your students to reflect on the research process. Ask them to think about everyday problems around the school that might be solved by using this process. List examples of these.

Problems

1. The class supply of erasers is being used up too fast.
2. Younger students never seem to get a turn on playground equipment.
3. Lots of litter is blowing around the schoolyard.

Solving the Problems

Now let's try to solve the problems.

Begin with a **statement of purpose** or a question.

Predict some solutions.

Gather some information (survey, collect, experiment ...).

Organize the results (chart, graph, classify, arrange, group ...).

Analyse the data (talk, look for patterns, interpret, compare with predictions ...).

Synthesize (answer the question, create solutions).

Apply (use the solution, apply the knowledge learned).

Evaluate the effectiveness of the solution.

Question Starters for Problems

☆ How can we ...?
☆ Is it possible to ...?
☆ What is the best way to ...?
☆ What are the chances of ...?

Now your students are becoming not only lifelong learners but also problem solvers.

Student Portfolios

Student portfolios can be useful in promoting student reflection. Encourage your students to collect an assortment of different work in their portfolios. You will want to set aside time regularly so that students can examine carefully what they have done, by

☆ thinking about their pieces
☆ making some decisions
☆ setting their personal goals
☆ planning new learning

Reflection Starters

These reflection starters will get your students thinking:

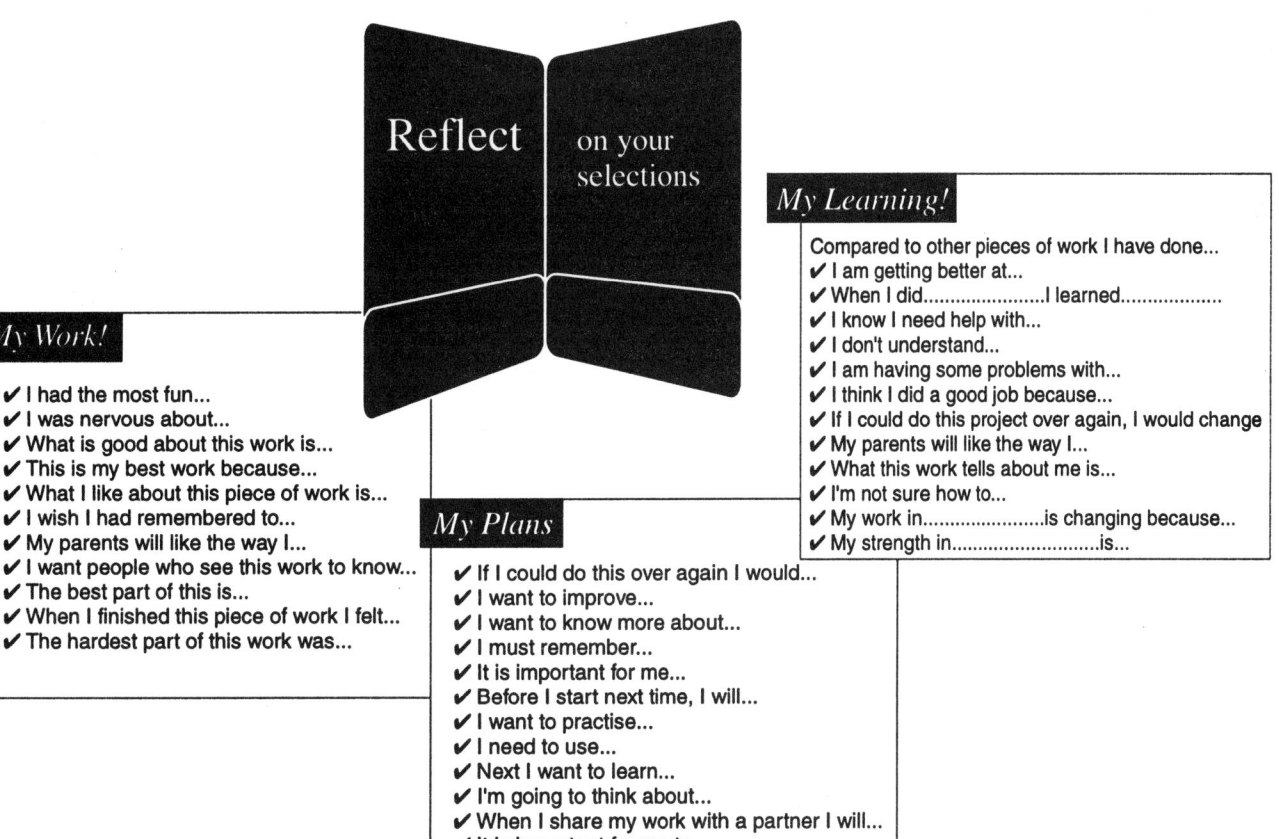

Reflect on your selections

My Work!
- ✔ I had the most fun...
- ✔ I was nervous about...
- ✔ What is good about this work is...
- ✔ This is my best work because...
- ✔ What I like about this piece of work is...
- ✔ I wish I had remembered to...
- ✔ My parents will like the way I...
- ✔ I want people who see this work to know...
- ✔ The best part of this is...
- ✔ When I finished this piece of work I felt...
- ✔ The hardest part of this work was...

My Learning!
Compared to other pieces of work I have done...
- ✔ I am getting better at...
- ✔ When I did.....................I learned..................
- ✔ I know I need help with...
- ✔ I don't understand...
- ✔ I am having some problems with...
- ✔ I think I did a good job because...
- ✔ If I could do this project over again, I would change
- ✔ My parents will like the way I...
- ✔ What this work tells about me is...
- ✔ I'm not sure how to...
- ✔ My work in.....................is changing because...
- ✔ My strength in...........................is...

My Plans
- ✔ If I could do this over again I would...
- ✔ I want to improve...
- ✔ I want to know more about...
- ✔ I must remember...
- ✔ It is important for me...
- ✔ Before I start next time, I will...
- ✔ I want to practise...
- ✔ I need to use...
- ✔ Next I want to learn...
- ✔ I'm going to think about...
- ✔ When I share my work with a partner I will...
- ✔ It is important for me to...

Reflection Tools

Sharing Reflections

Students can use organizers to focus their reflection on the learning process they undertook while producing pieces (a) individually and (b) with a partner. They can record what they learned and what they want to improve.

```
Name .................................................................
Reflection piece ......................... Date .................
I have included this piece because ...........................
.......................................................................
.......................................................................
I want you to know that ...........................................
.......................................................................
.......................................................................
When I did this I learned .........................................
.......................................................................
I want to work on improving .....................................
.......................................................................
```

```
Reflection piece ......................... Date .................
Partners ..............................................................
.......................................................................
This work shows that ...............................................
.......................................................................
.......................................................................
We discovered .......................................................
.......................................................................
We wonder ............................................................
.......................................................................
```

Conferencing

This sheet (page 105) provides students with pointers on the Who, How and When of conferencing.

Working Together

Students will find ideas about (a) when working in a group is most profitable and (b) the important roles individuals in a group can adopt (page 106).

At Home

Included here is vital information on (a) playing and winning the Homework Game — page 107; (b) how students can set up a supportive homework space — page 108; (c) what they can do and how their parents can help them link learning to life when there isn't any homework — page 109. You can hand out this take-home sheet as part of your encouragement to parents and students to take advantage of learning opportunities in the community.

Conferencing

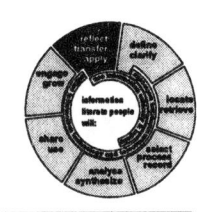

Who?

- ✔ learning partners
- ✔ teacher
- ✔ teacher-librarian
- ✔ parents / guardians

How?

Prepare to discuss the writing / product before each conference.

Share your work / product and your learning.

Practise critical reading / viewing and listening skills.

Reflect

Sit with your partner/s

When?

- ✔ Prewriting
- ✔ Editing
- ✔ Portfolios
- ✔ Reflection
- ✔ Celebrating
- ✔ Evaluating

Working Together

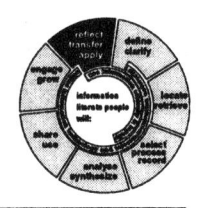

It is sometimes better to work in a group to

☆ brainstorm
☆ conference
☆ solve problems
☆ make decisions
☆ do computer activities
☆ design
☆ create
☆ construct
☆ experiment
☆ research
☆
☆

Everyone in a group has an important role to play.

All group members must be responsible for their own role.

If all group members do their job, learning is fun.

BRAINstorming

Strategies
✓ use IDEAS

Topic:
Group members:

I nvite lots of ideas
D efer decisions
E xpand!
A ccept all suggestions
S tretch your thinking

Brainstorming is a thinking exercise.
It is a way of getting lots and lots of ideas in a hurry.
It is a way of creating new ideas.
You can brainstorm: by yourself
with a friend
in small groups
with your class
Record all your ideas on paper, charts, chalk board, sticky notes, computer ...

Checker's Job

Have I written down everyone's ideas?
Does everyone understand?
Can everyone explain the answers?

Worrier's Job

Do we agree on what to do?
Are we doing what was asked?
Is everyone helping?

Encourager's Job

Am I keeping the group on track?
Am I smiling and giving others a thumbs-up?
Am I saying "Good idea!", "Let's go for it!", "Great job!"?

The Homework Game

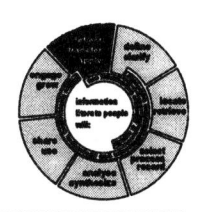

Play the Homework Game and WIN at school.

START — SCHOOL

- I write down homework as soon as it is assigned.
- I make sure I understand the homework before I leave school.
- I ask my teacher for help when I don't understand.
- I have a learning partner I can phone if I am away from school or if I don't fully understand an assignment.

HOME

- Shhh.... I have a quiet place to work.
- I avoid distractions from phone calls, television, etc.
- I do my homework early in the evening before I am too tired.
- I look after myself and take breaks when I need them.
- I keep my notebooks, folders and portfolios well organized.
- My homework is packed by the door ready for me to take to school.
- I hand in assignments on time.
- I reflect on my work... How could I do better? How will I use this learning?

107

Your Homework Space

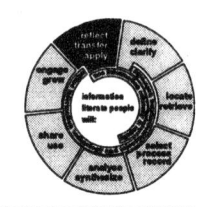

You need a place to work at home.

Discover the type of environment that works best for you.

- ✔ Create your own space away from other activities.
- ✔ Try propping books up at an angle.
- ✔ Use a planner to manage your time. 
- ✔ Make your space your own
    - posters
    - pictures
    - bulletin board
- ✔ Use a knapsack
    - organize it before you go to bed
    - include all your materials for the next day
    - put it by the door

If you need Music!
- ✔ try no lyrics
- ✔ keep it soft

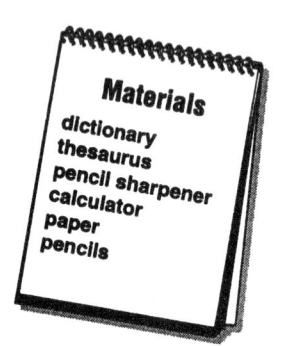

Materials
- dictionary
- thesaurus
- pencil sharpener
- calculator
- paper
- pencils

Link Learning to Life

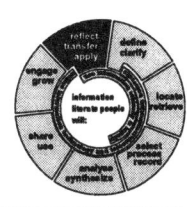

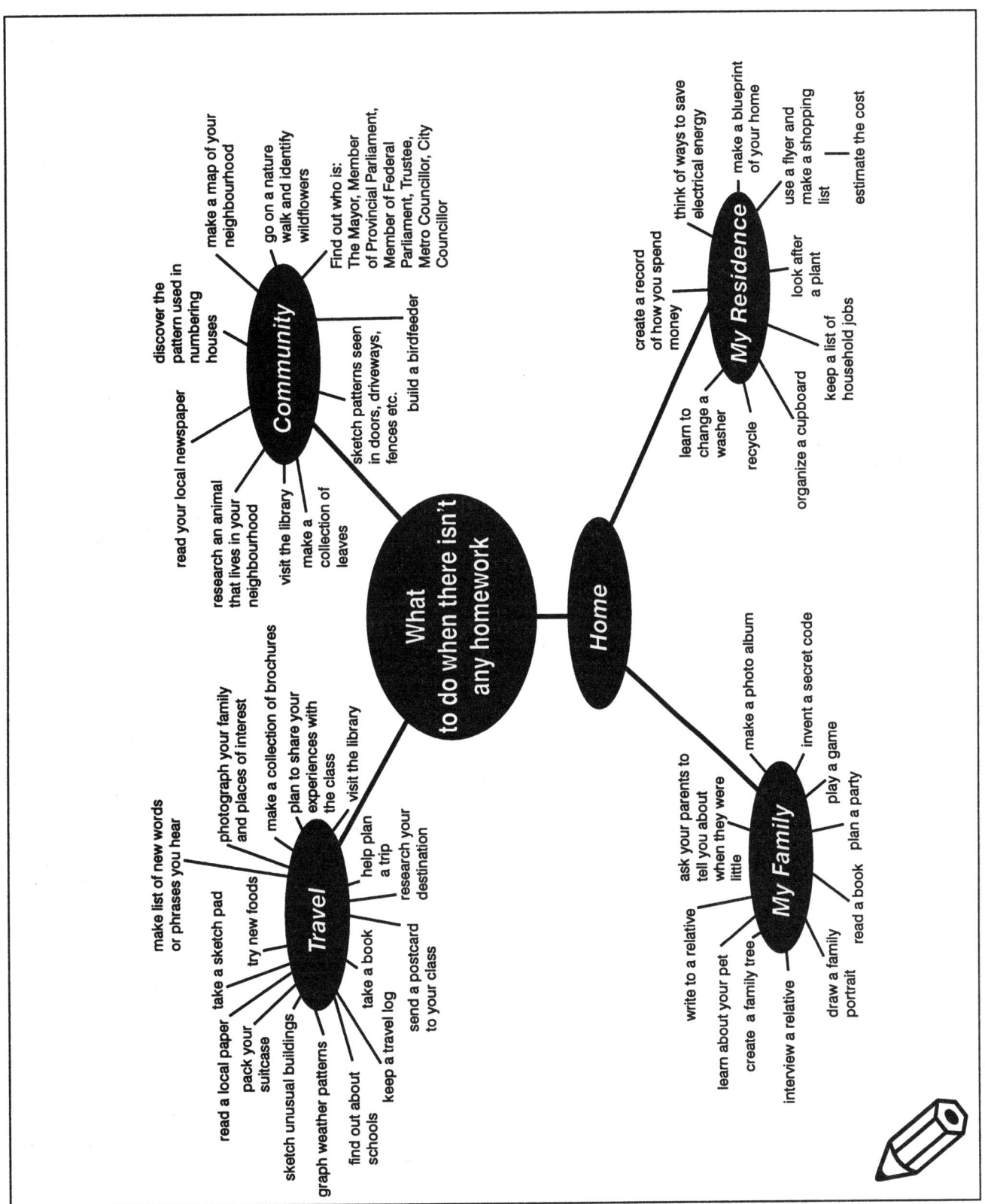

What to do when there isn't any homework

Community
- make a map of your neighbourhood
- go on a nature walk and identify wildflowers
- discover the pattern used in numbering houses
- Find out who is: The Mayor, Member of Provincial Parliament, Member of Federal Parliament, Trustee, Metro Councillor, City Councillor
- sketch patterns seen in doors, driveways, fences etc.
- build a birdfeeder
- make a collection of leaves
- visit the library
- research an animal that lives in your neighbourhood
- read your local newspaper

My Residence
- make a blueprint of your home
- think of ways to save electrical energy
- use a flyer and make a shopping list
- estimate the cost
- look after a plant
- keep a list of household jobs
- organize a cupboard
- recycle
- learn to change a washer
- create a record of how you spend money

Home

My Family
- make a photo album
- invent a secret code
- play a game
- plan a party
- ask your parents to tell you about when they were little
- read a book
- draw a family portrait
- interview a relative
- create a family tree
- learn about your pet
- write to a relative

Travel
- photograph your family and places of interest
- make a collection of brochures
- plan to share your experiences with the class
- visit the library
- help plan a trip
- research your destination
- send a postcard to your class
- keep a travel log
- take a book
- try new foods
- take a sketch pad
- make list of new words or phrases you hear
- pack your suitcase
- sketch unusual buildings
- read a local paper
- find out about schools
- graph weather patterns

109

Tracking and Evaluation

Students need to know up front what the learning expectations are. At the onset

☆ Define your criteria.
☆ Design a rubric.

Student Self- and Peer Evaluation

The group evaluation and research evaluation worksheets on pages 111 and 112 will assist individual students in reflecting on their progress in the research process, their enjoyment of this process and ways in which they can improve their learning.

Page 113 provides a formative assessment tool students can use in thinking about their progress as self-directed, information-literate learners. On page 114 you will find a vehicle for tracking your students' developing abilities in information accessing.

Tip

Students can apply their knowledge of fractions as they self-evaluate:

Shade in the pies below to show how well YOU thought you worked on each activity.

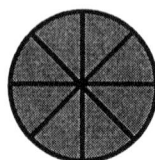

Outstanding!   Good!   Fair!   Needs Improvement!

How Well Is My Group Doing?

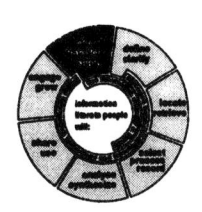

Here are some suggestions for evaluating your group work.

accept responsibility for your task

We support each other by ...

1] _____

2] _____

We make sure we stay on task by ...

1] _____

2] _____

Our team could improve by ...

1] _____

2] _____

I think we should try to _____

The best thing about group work is _____

Name.................................... Date....................

111

Evaluating My Research

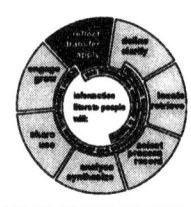

How did I do?

☹ 😐 ☺

Focus
① ② ③ ④ ⑤

I explored my topic. . . . .

I knew exactly what I needed to find out. . . . .

Process Data

I selected appropriate subtopics. . . . .

I selected an appropriate organizer . . . .

I found good sources of information. . . . .

I used dot-jots to record my information. . . . .

I kept a source sheet . . . .

I assessed my information . . . .

Product

I summarized my information . . . .

I created new ideas . . . .

I shared / used my learning. . . . .

Learning

My research skills are . . . .

My effort on this assignment was . . . .

I made good use of my time. . . . .

What I enjoyed most about doing this project was . . . .
. . . .

My goals for improvement are:

1. . . . .

2. . . . .

3. . . . .

Name . . . . Date . . . .

My Learning — How Am I Doing?

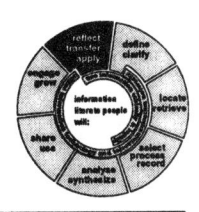

In the unit on _____

I am responsible for my own learning.

	Most of the time	Sometimes	Hardly ever	Not yet
I can listen well to the teacher and students when they read or speak.	❑	❑	❑	❑
I can view pictures, films, videos to find information.	❑	❑	❑	❑
I can read books to find information.	❑	❑	❑	❑
I can use computers to find information.	❑	❑	❑	❑
I can talk about my new learning.	❑	❑	❑	❑
I ask questions when I need help.	❑	❑	❑	❑
I am helpful to others.	❑	❑	❑	❑
I try to figure out things for myself.	❑	❑	❑	❑
I keep all my work in my research folder.	❑	❑	❑	❑
I can create something new with my information.	❑	❑	❑	❑

Name.. Date....................

Tracking Students' Abilities

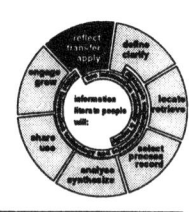

Student _____

The student can	Often	Sometimes	Hardly ever	Not yet
Respond to story	❏	❏	❏	❏
Listen to gather information	❏	❏	❏	❏
View to gather information	❏	❏	❏	❏
Read to gather information	❏	❏	❏	❏
Develop questions on topic	❏	❏	❏	❏
Record answers to questions	❏	❏	❏	❏
Organize gathered information pictorially	❏	❏	❏	❏
Organize gathered information textually	❏	❏	❏	❏
Work in a group to plan a sharing presentation	❏	❏	❏	❏
Create something new with her/his learning	❏	❏	❏	❏
Self-evaluate his/her learning	❏	❏	❏	❏

Teacher .... Date ....

At Each Stage ...

Use of Information Technologies and Telecommunication Networks

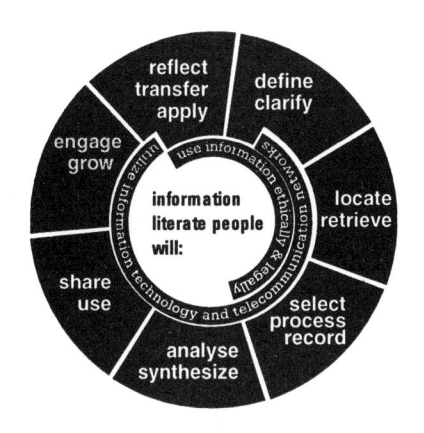

Throughout the research process, students will use information technologies and telecommunication networks. Primary students will need guidance and assistance in doing so.

Students will access information electronically from CD-ROMs and databases, using a variety of search criteria, including keywords and Boolean operations.

Students will locate and utilize electronic bulletin boards and the Internet (especially the World-Wide Web).

Students will use a computer to process information by

☆ selecting the right software
☆ using a word processor application
☆ utilizing clip art and drawing features
☆ creating charts and graphs

They will use a computer to share information by

☆ publishing their work
☆ including graphics, sound and video in multimedia presentations
☆ using E-mail and the Internet

Students will use information ethically and legally by

☆ following copyright and plagiarism laws and guidelines
☆ adequately referencing all their sources
☆ saving printouts in their research folders
☆ including references when they use someone else's work

Use the Power of Technologies

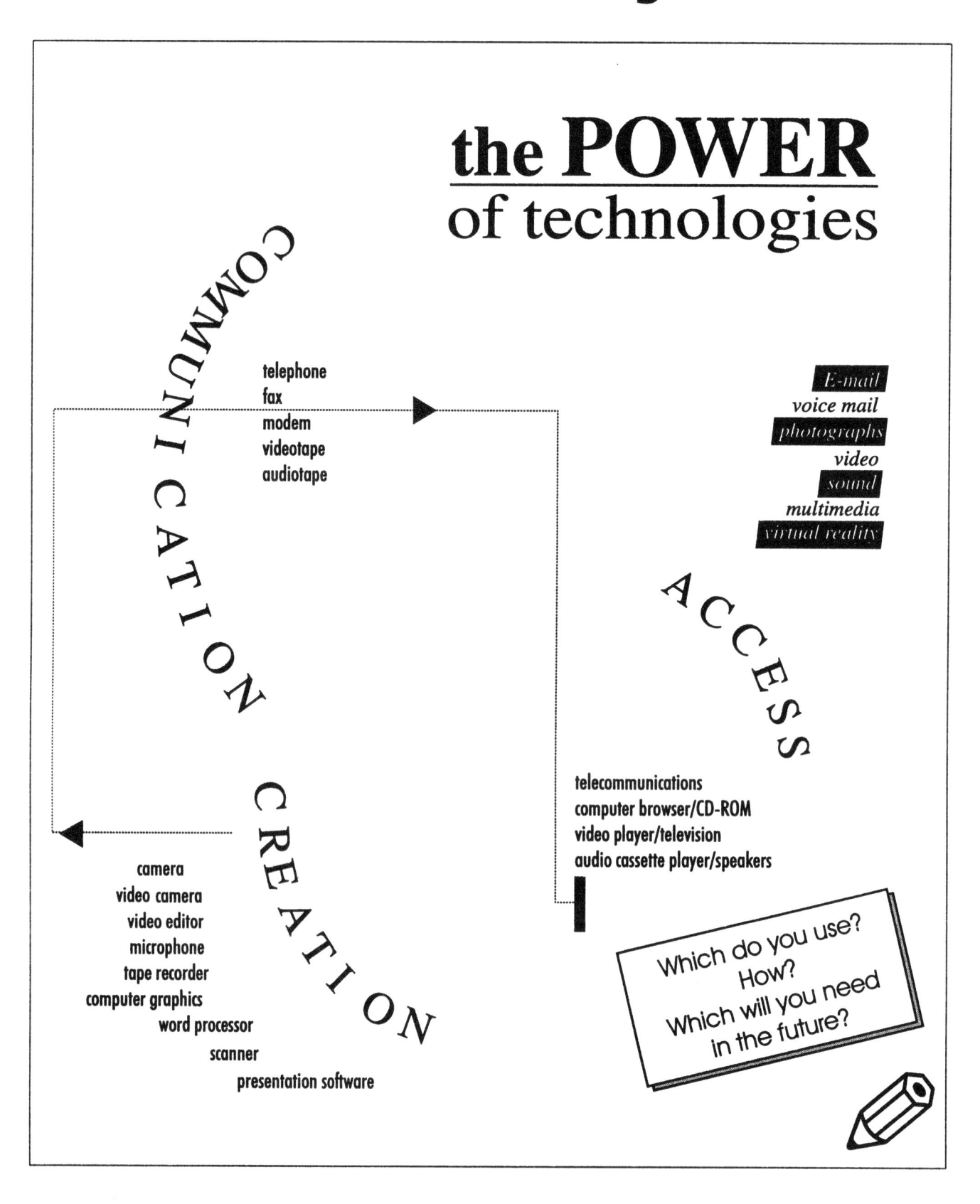

the POWER of technologies

COMMUNICATION

telephone
fax
modem
videotape
audiotape

E-mail
voice mail
photographs
video
sound
multimedia
virtual reality

ACCESS

telecommunications
computer browser/CD-ROM
video player/television
audio cassette player/speakers

CREATION

camera
video camera
video editor
microphone
tape recorder
computer graphics
word processor
scanner
presentation software

Which do you use?
How?
Which will you need in the future?

Using Technologies to Enhance Learning

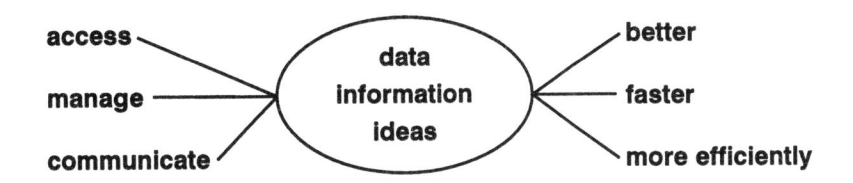

```
access ─╮                    ╭─ better
        ╰→ ⬭ data           ←╯
manage ──→   information   ←── faster
        ╭→   ideas         ←╮
communicate ╯                ╰─ more efficiently
```

Technologies are an integral part of the way we learn, work and play. Students need to know how to use the wide range of available technologies and educational tools. Once they have mastered the mechanics of the equipment, they require guidance in applying it to enhance their learning.

Students may know the various technologies available to them but need to learn

☆ which one meets their specific needs
☆ how to optimize the use of the technology
☆ when to use the technology

Does this technology help the students to

☆ use search tools to locate and retrieve?
☆ evaluate or analyse information?
☆ solve problems?
☆ apply new skills or knowledge?
☆ gain understanding?
☆ increase their independence?
☆ develop collaborative skills?

The efficient use of a technology often depends on what student have done in preparation. For example:

When **phoning** for information, students will be more successful if they have a prepared script and an organizer for recording.

If students have a clearly defined need and some good keywords, they are much more likely to be successful in searching the **Internet**.

Using a repertoire of search strategies on an **automated library catalogue** enables students to spend less time searching and more time processing information.

Comparing Technologies

Let's use the powerful focus word **compare**. Give your students opportunities to compare the efficiency and effectiveness of technologies and tools. For example:

Compare two different CD-ROM encyclopedias. Use the information in this organizer to help in analysing the usefulness of the CD-ROMs.

Note the strong points of each. Note the weaknesses of each. Which one did the best job?

Criteria	Encyclopedia	Encyclopedia
© Copyright Data		
Type of Search (keyword, Boolean, topic ...)		
Article Is it useful to me? Does it meet my needs?		
Links to related articles		
Visuals (pictures, video clips, charts, maphs, graphs)		
Structure Fonts, icons, HELP tools, layout		
Notepad Features		
Printing and Downloading		
My Analysis		

Show your students how to design their own organizers and develop criteria to compare other kinds of resources, such as books, videos, camcorder, video, slide show, software, CD-ROM, television, audio recording, E-mail, fax, Internet Web sites, search engines ...

Students should consider all the available tools and technologies and select the most appropriate. Sometimes traditional tools and resources are more effective and efficient.

The worksheets on the following pages supply essential information and tips that will help your students in using computer technologies effectively, efficiently and ethically.

Technical Tips

Make use of your word processing tools.

SAVE TO A DISK

Editing
- cut, copy, paste for revisions
- spell check
- utilize style and font features

Formatting
- set margins
- double space
- insert page number
- insert footer (date and file ID)

Enhancements
- create graphs, charts
- import clip art
- create and include sound, drawings, video clips

Remember: Work on content first. Then enhance it using word processing tools.

Title
Your First Name, Middle Name, Last Name
Your School

Teachers Name
Subject
Due date of written assignment

Click on a CD-ROM

Because you can store great amounts of information on a CD-ROM — especially important if you have sound, movies, or pictures — they've become the best way to deliver certain kinds of information.

Here's how to get started using a CD-ROM.

For External Drive
✔ Turn on your CD-ROM drive.

For Internal Drive
✔ Start or Re-start your Computer.

✔ Hold the CD by its edges only.
(If your CD-ROM drive requires a caddy, place the CD in the caddy with the label up.)

✔ Insert the caddy or CD in the CD-ROM drive with the label facing up.

✔ When the CD icon appears on the desktop, double-click on it to Open.

✔ To start the program, double-click on the main icon.

Note: Some programs will need a Web browser or a floppy disk to start. They may also require an amplified speaker or headphones.

Be WEBwise

©opyright

CANADA
http://insight.mcmaster.ca/org/efc/

USA
http://www.yahoo.com/government/law/intellectual-property/copyrights/

Keep your password, phone number and address confidential.
If you receive any information that makes you feel uncomfortable, tell an adult.
Never share your account.
Assume all material on the Net has copyright, even though the symbol © doesn't appear.

:-) Smiley
:-(Frown
;-) Wink
;-D Big Smile
:-() Ouch!
:-O WOW!

✔ Be polite.

✔ Use language that is not offensive.

✔ Use clear and concise language.

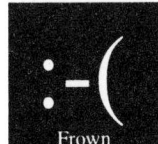

✔ Type messages in lowercase letters. Capital letters indicate Shouting or Yelling.

✔ Answer your E-mail messages promptly.

✔ Observe copyright and plagiarism conventions.

✔ Watch your time.

✔ Be fair and share.

✔ Download files in nonpeak hours when possible.

✔ Show consideration and respect for other users.

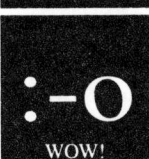

✔ Use online time efficiently
  - define your need
  - plan your path

✔ Get permission before you share personal E-mail messages.

✔ Observe your school's code of conduct or behaviour.

Words for the WEBwise

Address	see **URL**
Browser	software — (program) that lets you search/access a **Web** site (such as Netscape® Communicator, Microsoft® Internet Explorer)
Domain	last part of an E-mail address which indicates the type of user (such as .org or .com)
Download	to copy data from another computer
E-Mail	**electronic mail** sent and received by computers
Hypertext	underlined or highlighted Web site words that link you to another Web site or page when you click on them
LAN	**local area network** — a computer network at a single location (for example, rooms in your school)
Netiquette	manners for network users
Password	a secret code of letters and/or numbers that allows you access
Search Engine	a computer program that helps you find a site on the Internet (for example, Lycos or Yahoo Canada)
ISP	**Internet Service Provider** — a company paid to allow you to use its servers to access the Internet
Service Provider	see **ISP**
Surfing	moving from Web site to Web site searching and locating digital information
URL	**Uniform Resource Locator** — an address for a Web site
WWW	**World-Wide Web** — part of the Internet where you can select (pick) a site by clicking on graphics and hypertext
WAN	**Wide Area Network** — a computer network extending beyond a single site (for example, all the schools in your area)
Web site	a location on the WWW with information, pictures and sound, accessible using a Web browser

© Copyright Alert

Note each source on your Source Sheet. It's important to acknowledge when you've used someone else's work in your project. It's dishonest if you don't.

Plagiarism is...
... stealing the ideas, words, writings, etc. of someone else and passing them off as your own.
... breaking copyright laws.

- Avoid suspicion.
- Be aware of copyright laws.
- Give credit to others' work by including proper referencing.
- Keep printouts in your research folder.
- Make sure your work is original.
- Start with a research question or statement of purpose.

When you use others' works, give credit to the authors by proper referencing. All ideas, quotes, paraphrases, summaries, pictures, charts, maps and diagrams must be acknowledged by text citations and in the reference list at the end.

What is copyright?

✔ Copyright is the exclusive legal right to reproduce, publish and sell the matter and form.
✔ The categories of copyright governed by the law are: audio-visual, literary (including computer software), musical (including sound recordings), dramatic and artistic.
✔ Copyright protects both creators and users. If creators never get paid for their work, they will eventually stop producing.

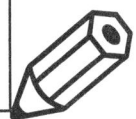

Computer Learning Log

Each software application you can learn to use makes it easier for you to learn another. You might want to keep track of the version you're using and note the features that change in the next version.

You may want to create your own log on the computer.

Untitled - Notepad

File Edit Search Help   _____'s Computer Log

Application/Version	Date	I did/used	I need help with . . .	I want to learn to . . .

In Conclusion

To succeed — and have fun — in the rapidly changing information age, students must prepare themselves with the knowledge, skills and values that they'll need in tomorrow's world of work and pleasure.

We hope that using *Teaching Tools* will help guide your students in becoming information-literate lifelong learners. Through exploration and practice, they will be ready to meet successfully — and enjoy — the challenges of the information revolution.

Related Resources

Andersen, Neil (1989). *Media Works*. Toronto, ON: Oxford University Press.

Booth, David (1996). *Literacy Techniques for Building Successful Readers and Writers*. Markham, ON: Pembroke Publishers Limited.

Breivik, Patricia Senn and J.A. Senn (1994). *Information Literacy: Educating Children for the 21st Century*. New York: Scholastic Inc.

Carroll, Jim and Donald Galbraith (1997). *Surviving in the Information Age*. Scarborough, ON: Prentice Hall Canada.

Cecil, Nancy Lee (1995). *The Art of Inquiry*. Winnipeg: Peguis Publishers.

Fogarty, Robin; Carla Bellanca Kahler; Sharon Nowakowski, editors (1990). *The Cooperative Think Tank: Graphic Organizers to Teach Thinking in the Cooperative Classroom*. Palatine, IL: IRI/Skylight Publishing, Inc.

Fogarty, Robin (1991). *The Mindful School: How to Integrate the Curricula*. Palatine, IL: Skylight Publishing, Inc.

Galbraith, Donald et al (1997). *Analyzing Issues*. Toronto: Trifolium Books Inc.

Gardiner, Howard and Donald Galbraith (1995). *Multiple Intelligences*. New York: Basic Books (HarperCollins).

Garfield, Gary and Suzanne McDonough (1995). *Modems, Megabytes and Me*. Winnipeg: Peguis Publishers.

Gawith, Gwen and Donald Galbraith (1987). *Information Alive!* Auckland: Longman Paul Limited.

Lake, Jo-Anne (1997). *Lifelong Learning Skills*. Markham, ON: Pembroke Publishers Limited.

Metropolitan Toronto School Board (1996). *Getting It All Together: Curriculum Integration for the Transition Years*. Markham, ON: Pembroke Publishers Limited.

Moline, Steve (1995). *I See What You Mean: Children at Work with Visual Information*. Markham, ON: Pembroke Publishers Limited.

Worsnop, Chris M. (1996). *Assessing Media Work*. Mississauga, ON: Wright Communications.

Index

Action plan, for research, 8, 9, 11
Analysis/synthesis, 55-57
Assessment, self-, 53
Audience/purpose, in writing, 74
Audio-video resources, 39
Boolean searches, 27, 115
Brainstorming
　in preresearch, 16
　recalling information, 58
Browsers, computer, 25-27, 115, 116
CD-ROM
　databases, 25-27, 115, 116
　encyclopedias, comparing, 118
　using, 120
Characters, in story, 83, 84, 86
Charts/diagrams, types of, 62-64
Clustering, 17
Communication technologies, 115-117
Community, 52, 109
Compare/contrast, 92, 93
Computer learning log, 124
Computer skills, 117-118, 119, 124
Computer software, 118, 119
Conclusions, 51-52, 53-56
Connections, making, 80, 86
Cooperation, 106, 111
Copyright, 35, 53, 115, 123
Critical thinking, 56, 96, 101
　in text evaluation, 56, 96
Cross-classification chart, 64
Curriculum, developing, 6
Data
　checking quality, 28, 35, 112
　comparing, 51, 54
　defined, 7
　in intellectual access to information, 7
　recording, 45-46
　selecting/processing, 35-36
　validity of, 28
Data analysis, 55-57
Data search, focusing/organizing, 22
Databases, types of, 25-27, 115, 116
Decision making, 96
Diagrams/charts, types of, 62-64
Dot-jot notes (point form), 46
Draft, first/second, 74
E-mail, 115, 116, 118
Economy, knowledge, 5
Editing writing, 74, 75-76
Electronic information systems, 25-27, 115, 116

Encyclopedias, comparing CD-ROMs, 118
Ethical use of information, 35, 53, 115, 123
Evaluating research, 35, 50, 112
Evaluation
　peer, 110, 111
　self-, 53, 110, 113
　of student abilities, 114
Facts
　and fiction, 44-45
　and opinions, 28, 53
Family, 52, 109
Film catalogues, 25-26
Filmstrips, 25
Fluency/flexibility, in thinking, 96
Focusing on a topic, 18
Format, for presentations, 67, 71-73
Genres, literary/media, 77, 79
Goals, setting, 85
Graphic analysers, for literary/media text, 80, 87, 91, 94, 97
Graphic organizers, 56, 59-64
Group work, 106, 111
　evaluating, 102
Homework, 107-108
　when there isn't any, 109
Human resources, 25-27, 34, 54
Ideas
　brainstorming, 16
　clustering, 17
　webbing, 15, 16, 17
Information, 5, 7, *see also* Data
　analysis/synthesis, 55-57
　audio-visual, 39
　collecting (KNL model), 42-43
　defined, 7
　ethical use of, 35, 123
　intellectual access to, 6, 7
　physical access to, 6
　tools for accessing, 23
Information centre, 25-27
Information literacy, 5
　planning for integration, 11
Information organizer, 45
Inquiry question, 16, 18-21
Intelligences, multiple, 67-68, 72
Internet, in research, 25, 26, 117
Interviewing, 32, 34
Kaleidoscope, as analysis/synthesis metaphor, 57
Keywords, identifying, 18-19

KNL model, collecting information, 19, 42-43
Knowledge, in intellectual access to information, 7
Learning
　applying, 100-110
　linking to life, 109
　making personal/skills connections, 100, 101, 104
　sharing, 65, 66, 70, 72
　skills for, 7
　transferring, 101
　working together, 106, 111
Learning Expectations, 8, 24, 35, 57, 65, 79, 100, 115
Learning log, computer, 124
Librarian, teacher-
　as human resource, 25-27
　student conferencing with, 105
Library
　card catalogue, 27
　locating/retrieving resources, 25-27, 29, 30-31
　public, 31
Life, linking learning to, 109
Lifelong learning, skills for, 6
Listening, active, 38
Literary experiences, 79-97
Literature
　characters, 83, 84
　decision making, 96
　fluency/flexibility, 96
　personal response to story, 82
　problem solving, 86, 88, 90, 95
　reading log, 81
　selection criteria, 80, 83
　setting/time, 82
　types/genres, 80
Magazine/newspaper indexes, 24-27
Mapping, story, 87, 91
Media, deconstructing, 94
Media log, 81
Microscope, as analysis/synthesis metaphor, 57
Mind map, 15
Multimedia presentations, 64-66, 69
Multiple intelligences, 67-68, 72
Narrowing the topic, 22
Newspaper indexes, 24-27
Note making, 46
Opinions, and facts, 28, 53
Oral presentations, 67, 71-73

Organizers, graphic, 45-50, 52
    taste test, 80
Personal meaning, 80
Personal response, to story, 82
Personal strengths, 69, 80, 85
Pictures, reading, 36-37
Plagiarism, 35, 53, 115, 123
Planning, teacher, 11-13
Point form, to record data, 46
Portfolio, student reflection, 103
Predicting story events, 86, 88, 89
Presentation
    evaluating, 112, 113
    multimedia, 67, 71-73
    oral/written/visual, 67, 71-73
    planning, 69
    selecting a format, 67, 71-73
Presentation cube, 73
Presentation rubric, 78
Problem solving
    literature, 86, 88, 90, 95
    skills transference, 102
Process/product, reflecting, 100
Purpose/audience, in writing, 74
Quality, checking for, 28, 50, 56
Questioning
    older students, 19-21
    preresearch, 16, 18
    younger students, 18-19
Questions, answering/sharing
    learning, 66
Reading, 40
Reading log, 81
Recording data, 45-46
Reference list, *see* Source(s)
Reflecting, 15, 103
Reflection starters/tools, 103
Research
    folder, starting, 23
    organizing, 45-50, 52
    success, planning for, 8
Resources
    audio-visual, 39
    checklist, 28
    comparing/choosing, 114
    evaluating, 29
    human, 25-27, 34, 54
    locating/retrieving, 24-25

Response journal, 82, 83
Revising writing, 74, 75-76
Scanning, 26
Searches
    Boolean, 27, 115
    keyword, 27
Self-assessment, 53
Self-awareness skills, 69, 80, 85
Self-improvement, 100
Self-knowledge, 68, 69, 80, 85
Series line, 62
Setting, story, 82, 85
Sharing
    new learning, 65, 66, 70, 72
    talents, 72
Skimming, 26
Solutions, finding, 86, 88, 90
Source(s)
    checking, 28, 35, 112
    listing, 54
    recording, 53, 54
Source sheets, 54
Steps to success, 14
Storyboard, in writing process, 77
Strengths/weaknesses, 68, 69, 80, 85
Student progress, tracking, 110, 114
Study tips, 107-108
Subtopics, to focus/organize data
    search, 22
Surveying, 32-33
Synthesizing information, 55-57
Talents, hidden, 68, 69, 80, 85
Taste, in genre, 80
Taste test, 80
Teacher
    curriculum development, 5
    information literacy facilitation, 6
    planning, 11-13
    role in the research process, 9-10
    tracking, 14
    tracking student abilities, 114
Teacher-librarian, *see* Librarian,
    teacher-
Technological literacy, 115-117
Technologies
    comparing, 118
    Internet, 25, 26, 117
    power of, 116

    telephone, 117
Telling, in preresearch, 16
Theme/Topic, integration vehicle, 6
3T chart, 63
Time, organizing, 107-108
Time line, 62
Toffler, Alvin, 5
Topic
    focusing on, 18, 20-22, 60
    narrowing, 19, 22
Transferring/applying learning,
    100-110
Transferring skills, critical thinking,
    101
T chart, 59, 63
Tree diagram, 56, 64
Tri-Venn diagram, 56, 63
Venn diagram, 43, 56, 63
Video
    in the curriculum, 98
    developing skills, 98
Video catalogues, 25-26
Viewing, 39
Visual presentations, 67, 71-73
Web diagram, 15, 16, 17, 62
Web, World-Wide
    terms, 122
    wise/ethical use of, 121
Webbing ideas, 15, 16, 17
Wide angle lens, as analysis/synthesis
    metaphor, 57
Wisdom, in intellectual access to
    information, 7
Word processors, tips for using, 119
Work, world of, 5
Work area, organizing, 108
Working together, 99-100
    evaluating group work, 102
World-Wide Web, *see* Web,
    World-Wide
Writing
    purpose/audience, 74
    revising/editing, 74, 75-76
    tracking, 76
Writing process, steps in, 74
Written presentations, 67, 71-73